THE RULES OF THE GAME

Your Rights, The Criminal Justice System,

and Courtroom Procedure

Written by

J Scott Stevens

DISCLAIMER

The Material herein may contain inaccuracies or typographical errors. The author or Strand Investigations and Consulting, LLC make no representations about the accuracy, reliability, completeness or timeliness of the Material. The use of the Material is at your own risk. Changes are periodically made to the Material and may be made at any time and are provided on an "as is" basis without any warranties of any kind. The author and Strand Investigations and Consulting, LLC, to the fullest extent permitted by law, disclaims all warranties, whether express or implied, including the warranty of merchantability, fitness for particular purpose and non-infringement. The author and Strand Investigations and Consulting, LLC makes no warranties about the accuracy, reliability, completeness or timeliness of the Material, services, software, text, graphics and links.

All of the information contained herein is designed to provide accurate and authoritative information in regard to the subject matter covered. It is sold with the understanding that the publisher, the author, and Strand Investigations and Consulting, LLC are not engaged in rendering legal, accounting or any services other than those designated herein. If legal advice or other professional assistance is required, the services of a competent professional should be sought.

No part of this book may be resold, reproduced, stored in a retrieval system or transmitted in any form or by any means, electronic, mechanical, photocopying, recording or otherwise, without the prior written consent of the author and its owners. Any violation regarding the rights and singular use and benefit of intellectual property owned by the author and Strand Investigations and Consulting, LLC will be prosecuted to the fullest extent of the law.

Copyright ©2012 Strand Investigations and Consulting, LLC.
All rights reserved.

4

Table of Contents

Preface 11

Introduction 19

The Rules of the Game 21

    The 1st Amendment 22

    The 4th Amendment 27

        Warrantless Searches 42

        Warrantless Arrests 44

        Reasonable Suspicion and Probable Cause 46

        A Reasonable Expectation of Privacy 54

        Summarizing the 4th Amendment 64

    The 5th Amendment 66

        Good Cop, Bad Cop 70

        Field Sobriety Tests 73

    The 6th Amendment 80

        Miranda 87

        Excited Utterance 89

        The Hearsay Rule 92

    The Amendments Concluded 94

The Process of Arrest 97

    Custodial versus Non-Custodial 97

    Arrest Warrants 103

    Search Warrants 107

    Search Incident to an Arrest 116

    Terry Frisk or Pat Down 118

    Vehicle Inventory 121

    Protective Sweeps 124

    The Use of Police K-9 125

Other Things to Consider 131

    Constructive Possession 132

    Recording Devices 138

    Arguing Your Case in the Field 140

Courtroom Procedure 143

Pre-Trial Negotiation 144

Your Right to a Trial 147

The Process 152

    The Bench Trial 152

    The Jury Trial 167

General Strategies 171

    Argue the Facts 171

    Discredit the Witness 173

    Blame Someone Else 175

    Innocence, To Prove or Not To Prove 177

    Be the Prosecution 178

Rules of Evidence 181

    A Brady Motion 181

8

The Submission of Evidence	183
Be Professional	185
Conclusion	**189**

Preface

After having served in law enforcement for many years, it may seem strange to some that I endeavor to write a book designed to educate violators in ways that may enable them to defeat those charges in court. However, I always preferred a defendant who knew the law over one who didn't or a defendant who would present an argument to the charges in court. It kept me sharp and on my toes. It ensured that I always did a good job and that my cases were solid.

Now, some of my peers may disagree with this concept and think that I have violated some type of secret code by writing this book. Yet, I would argue that this book will serve to make them better officers.

The law as complex as it may appear, in its most simple form is nothing more than a game. The overriding point in this book is that one cannot expect to win the game if one does not know the rules. Now, rules are rules and they are not meant to be broken. However, you need to know where the line is so you can push the envelope without going so far as to break them. That is the game that the police play on a daily basis. We all do it in one form or another every day. We stretch the rules as far as we can while attempting not to stretch them so far they actually break.

Think of your yearly tax return. Don't we all search for even that slightest deduction that might mean a little bit higher refund check? We bend the rules to find that deduction but we do not go so far as to outright break them for fear of suffering the wrath of the IRS and an audit. Yet, the point I am trying to make remains, we all play the game.

How many of you drive the posted speed limit all the time? I would say that no one drives the speed limit, but I know there is someone out there that will insist that they "never" speed. Let me tell you something, the word "never" is a concept in the absolute, similar to saying "always". It does not leave any margin for error or any room for "but".

In any case, I digress from the topic at hand. So, for argument sake, the "vast majority" of us rarely drive at the posted speed limit. Of those, the majority drive somewhere within 6-8 mph of the posted speed limit. A smaller number of these people regularly drive 10-15 mph over the posted speed limit. An even smaller number regularly drive 16+ mph over the limit.

Regardless of where you might fall into this spectrum of speeding drivers, the point again is that we all play the game. Obviously, the majority of us who drive above the posted speed limit but within a smaller range of excess are a lot less likely to get into trouble versus those among us who regularly blow the envelope apart by driving to excessive speeds above the posted limits.

Now, one could certainly argue that 1 mph over the limit is breaking the law and thus not bending the rules. However, one could also argue that when something becomes a commonly accepted practice, that it replaces the written rule.

Think about it. The police rarely if ever stop a car travelling 1-5 mph over the posted speed limit, much less write a ticket for that level of offense. So, is the posted speed really the limit or is the actual limit 5 mph above what is posted? Either way, this is a philosophical discussion for another day, but I think I accomplished the first and primary task of this book, namely to make you think.

As we have already said, the rules are there not to be broken, but knowing where those limits are allows us to bend them. This is how the police use the rules and the law to their advantage. They know where the line is and operate as close to it as they can without crossing it. Most people know the general concepts of the rules governing our criminal justice system, but they do not know them well enough to push the envelope to their advantage. In this book, I attempt to explain the rules and show you how they work and are applied in a real sense. Therefore, you too may learn how to make the system work for you.

I don't mean to sound as though I am anti-police. As I stated at the outset, the fact is that I was a police officer for many years. I am still a police officer at heart and will always be. Yet, what I can't stand is the half-assed job that passes as quality police work today

So, a contrarian point of view might suggest that my teaching you the rules of the road so to speak will force the police to do their job better. I have been a firsthand witness to many cases where if the defendant had just possessed a basic understanding of their rights and the process, they could have easily won their case. Instead, the officer only has to offer a sloppy case and weak testimony to be victorious due to the defendant's ignorance.

Now, let me clarify that last statement about the defendant's ignorance before some of you close this book in disgust over my apparent disdain for the criminal defense.

Ignorance and stupidity are completely different things. Ignorance is not knowing. Stupidity is knowing but doing it anyway. I will be the first to admit that I have a low tolerance for stupidity. If you know something to be true, right, wrong, or whatever and still insist on doing the opposite, that is stupidity. Yet, I have a lot more patience for ignorance, because in that case a person just doesn't know. Until they do, how can they be held to a standard?

How many of you have ever been scolded as children for putting your feet on the furniture with your shoes on? You were usually warned several times before the wrath was bought down. The expectations were made clear through the warnings. It's not like on the very first instance your parent walked in and physically knocked you off the couch for your putting your feet on the furniture. On the other hand, if after being warned of the consequences you still insisted on putting your feet on the furniture, you demonstrated your stupidity and have no one to blame but yourself for the punishment you received. Do you see the difference?

In many cases, the police officer's success is based on their taking advantage of your ignorance. It is not their job to educate you on your rights and the rules of the system. There are hundreds, maybe thousands, of jail house lawyers who can attest to this. They received their education after numerous run ins with law enforcement and extensive experience in the criminal justice system. The problem is that they are often locked up in prison before they have figured the system out.

Learn the rules of the game and the process we call the criminal justice system before you get to that point. I certainly do not have to literally shoot myself to know that a gunshot wound is going to hurt. Likewise, you shouldn't have to go to jail or worse to learn how the criminal justice system works.

Our criminal justice system was established with a series of checks and balances, rules that officers and prosecutors must adhere to, and protections guaranteed to you the citizen. If one side of the system weakens, then the system is subject to corruption and failure. The police and prosecutors need to do their job well and that can only be guaranteed by an educated public. This is the underlying intent of this book, to educate you the public and thus strengthen the system overall.

Trying to change the police and force them to do a more quality job is literally fighting city hall. Not to mention the fact that the police culture has degraded over many years. The only true way to repair the system is for defendants to start winning cases based on poor police performance. Only then will they have to change their methods and once again start to bring forth good quality cases. For too long, the police have become accustomed to winning based on your ignorance. Your becoming educated about your rights and the criminal justice system ensures that everything is done more fairly, that justice is measured equally, and balance is restored to the system.

I hope you enjoy the book and learn more about the system that was designed to protect you the citizen.

INTRODUCTION

The court and legal process in general has been made to appear very complex, creating a need for those with advanced degrees in the law to help guide us through it. While this may be the case in many circumstances, just as many situations exist where this extra-ordinary level of expertise is not required in order to function and be successful within our legal system. However, a basic understanding of your rights, the legal process, fundamental rules of evidence and testimony, and basic strategy are required.

Now, this is not necessarily rocket science. In fact, police officers serve as the prosecutor in many jurisdictions for low level and municipal offenses. Though it is true that a police officer receives training in the law and the legal process, much of it involves elements of crimes, court room procedure, basic rules of evidence, and the civil rights contained within the United States Constitution. By no means are they an attorney, nor are they experts at criminal prosecution. To the contrary, a large number of cases are won because the defendant didn't have any basic understanding of the process where in some instances a simple question or two could have created the reasonable doubt necessary for a not guilty verdict.

I know that the process can appear intimidating, but at the end of the day, they are no better equipped than you can be given an understanding of some basic principles.

1

THE RULES OF THE GAME

You have several very important rights guaranteed to you under the United States Constitution. With the exception of your Miranda Warnings, which we will discuss a little later, the police are not required to make sure that you know and understand your rights as guaranteed in the Constitution. As a citizen of this country, it is your responsibility to be informed and know them for yourself.

In most academies, police candidates are grilled and tested on the Bill of Rights, so they know them frontward and backward. These are the rules for the game that they play in their pursuit of criminals. Breaking one of these rules usually results in an immediate dismissal of charges. Thus, you can see why it is so important for the police to know what the rules are.

But, how do you know if they have broken a rule if you don't know what the rules are? Or, you only know of them what you have seen on television? In addition, some of these rights are there to help you when your case goes to court. Again, if you don't know what they are and understand them, how are you to properly defend yourself or attain the protections to which you may be entitled.

This entire next section is dedicated to a discussion of the rules most common to the criminal justice system. As I have stated before, I am not an attorney and I do not pretend to be so. However, the rights contained in the United States Constitution are fairly straight forward. You do not have to possess a law degree to understand their basic intent and the protections they grant to you. Let's start our journey and take a look at what the rules are.

The 1st Amendment

The 1st Amendment is one that most people know simply as their right to freedom of speech. However, it is more than that. Let me quote it directly from the Constitution. Read it carefully:

> "Congress shall make no law respecting an establishment of religion, or prohibiting the free exercise thereof; or abridging the freedom of speech, or of the press; or the right of the people peaceably to assemble, and to petition the government for a redress of grievances."

The 1st Amendment not only guarantees your freedom of speech, but also your freedom of religion, your right to peacefully assemble, and the right to petition the government for redress of grievances.

Now, with these rights being guaranteed by the Constitution, you must also understand that these rights are not without limitations. Simply put, these rights are guaranteed so long as they do not endanger others or cause other's rights to be violated. For example, the old story of screaming "Fire!" in a crowded movie theater. This type of speech will not be protected by the 1st Amendment because it endangers the lives of others through the high probability of the panic that would be caused by that speech.

Your freedom of speech will not be protected if you tell someone that you are going to kill them and they believe your statement. Your speech may not be protected if you are cursing and using profanity in a loud boisterous manner on a crowded sidewalk where others can hear. Your rights have limitations. These limitations are created by everyone's equal and unalienable right to life, liberty, and the pursuit of happiness as stated in the United States Declaration of Independence.

While you maintain the rights to freedom of speech, freedom of religion, and freedom to peacefully assemble, these rights cannot be at the expense of another person and their rights. Does this make sense? It's not complicated if you think about it.

So, with this basic understanding, can you call a police officer a derogatory name or use some sort of derogatory gesture and expect it to be protected speech? As long as that speech was between you and the officer and an argument cannot be made that it negatively affected others, then probably.

Yet, just because you might be allowed to do something, does not mean you should. I would never advise anyone to disrespect a police officer or any other person in a position of authority as it only invites more problems than it's worth. Taking the legality out of the equation, if you made some kind of derogatory remark to your employer, how long do you think you will remain employed? If they don't fire you then, you can bet they will find a reason down the road. So, though you have certain protections, keep your wits about you and do not abuse your rights.

The right to peacefully assemble is the other point of interest within the 1st Amendment. I know a jurisdiction that will cite or arrest a person for standing on the sidewalk. Now, in part, I understand the problem the jurisdiction faces during busy times of the year and significant influxes of people. They are trying to maintain order in an almost uncontrollable situation. Yet, to disallow a person or a group of people from standing on the sidewalk seems to be a violation of the right to peacefully assemble guaranteed under the 1st Amendment. What do you think?

The argument to be made is that a person or persons standing on a sidewalk obstructs the use of that sidewalk by others and causes these others to have to step into the roadway to go around. The people blocking the sidewalk create a risk and a potential danger to those forced to step off the sidewalk and into the roadway to walk around.

I can see this as a problem infringing on the rights of others. In addition, as the sidewalk is a public conveyance, everyone should enjoy the same right to use it and not have their ability taken away by those who would stand and cause it to be blocked. However, what if the particular sidewalk is two or three squares wide, leaving ample room for other people to walk by without the need to step into the roadway? Do the original arguments still hold water? What if the people alleged to be blocking the sidewalk are only two and are not enough of a hindrance so as to prevent others from passing by freely without the need to step into the roadway? Do the original arguments still survive?

I would submit that they do not. To enforce a law such as the obstruction of passage for standing on a public sidewalk, barring any clearly identifiable hazards created by the action, is a direct violation of your 1st Amendment right to peacefully assemble. Maybe this is a stretch, but I believe there is an argument to be made. My point is that you need to examine your rights in light of the law and think about your situation. Don't just take things at face value.

The 4th Amendment

While the 1st Amendment was fairly easy to understand, the police spend a much greater amount of time learning and understanding the 4th Amendment. This one amendment is most central to their role as law enforcement and governs the majority of their actions and authority over the public. Just as they do, we will discuss the 4th Amendment in great detail. Numerous case laws already exist and new precedents are being set all the time concerning this one amendment. This one paragraph contains a lot of information and many gray areas. Thus, the reason it is arguably the most contested issue in criminal cases. Before delving too far into it, you can read it for yourself, but read it carefully:

> "The right of the people to be secure in their persons, houses, papers, and effects, against unreasonable searches and seizures, shall not be violated, and no warrants shall issue, but upon probable cause, supported by oath or affirmation, and particularly describing the place to be searched, and the persons or things to be seized."

Not too bad or complicated, right? Let's take a closer look at it, piece by piece:

> "The right of the people to be secure in their persons, houses, papers, and effects, against unreasonable searches and seizures, shall not be violated..."

This first statement is fairly straight forward, stating that a person is protected against *unreasonable* searches and seizures. Simply put, the police cannot just come into your home, they cannot just search your car, and they cannot just search your person. Similarly, the police cannot just seize your property or you in your person. While the aspects of both search and seizure described in the opening line of the 4th Amendment appear to be fairly straight forward, they each have been and continue to be argued in court as new cases present new issues.

Looking first at what may or may not constitute a legal search, I would ask how many times you think that a person with drugs in their possession willingly turn them over to the police when they are asked if they have drugs on them?

You would be surprised, a lot more that you would think. How many times do you think people give officers permission to search the contents of their pockets knowing that they are concealing drugs inside?

Again, it happens a lot more than you would think. Despite the many years I have worked the street, this never ceased to amaze me. They never had to tell me what was in their pockets, but people always do. The fact is that you never have to give consent for the police to search you, your home, or any of your property.

Now, I have heard the argument, "Well, you are the police. You would have found it anyway." That is the statement of ignorance. Make the police work for it. Don't do their job for them. If you do not give your consent, then they will have to find another way. If they cross the line and do it wrong, then you win in court.

Another clue is that if an officer is asking permission to search you, he or she doesn't have enough reason to search without your consent. Again, NEVER have to consent to a search. When I ask the people I have arrested under these circumstances, why they told me they had drugs on them or why they gave me permission to search their pockets when they knew I would find the drugs, their answers have always been one of two:

1. I figured you would find the drugs anyway.
2. I was calling your bluff and didn't think you would actually search me

Now, I am not so naïve as to think that there aren't officers out there who break the rules and who would conduct an illegal search. However, it is a weak case that leaves both the officer and their department open to significant liability. I like to believe that those officers are the exception and not the rule. As to the second explanation I have been given, don't ever call an officer's bluff on allowing him or her to search you, your car, your house, or anything. An officer would be a fool to turn down a free search where anything could be found.

In another example, let's say an officer wants to look at your cell phone for possible evidence of a crime ie, incriminating text messages, photos, call logs etc. Having spent a lot of time working with and around the 4th Amendment, an experienced officer is not going to ask to search your cell phone. More than likely, he or she will just ask to see the phone. If you willingly give it to them, you have in essence consented to their search of its contents.

You need to be aware of the game that is being played. It's really all in the wording and how things are perceived. You do not have to surrender the phone, much less let the officer look at its contents. The act of the officer taking the phone from you would constitute a seizure under the 4th Amendment and his looking through its contents would constitute a search. If you do not give your consent, neither is possible without the officer meeting a much higher burden or possibly even having to secure a warrant.

Let's look at another example, say a police officer knocks at the door of your home. When you answer the door, the officer asks to come in and speak with you. Do you have to let that officer in your home? What if the officer is walking in as he or she asks permission to come in and speak with you, can you stop the officer and refuse them entry to your home?

The answer to the first part is absolutely not. You do not have to let the police enter your home without a warrant (we will discuss warrants and warrantless searches a little later). As for the second part, you can certainly attempt to stop the officer from entering your home, telling them they do not have your permission to enter without a warrant.

I would not advise getting into a confrontation, but make sure that they know they have crossed the line and you know your rights. You need to make it clear that they are entering your home without your consent, but do not go so far as to get into a physical confrontation. Then, my next call would be to an attorney because your 4th Amendment rights have just been violated. I would even attempt to make the call immediately while the police are still present. The police really hate dealing with lawyers. Why? Because they know the rules of the game.

Now, consider the fact that we have only begun to touch upon the intricacies of the 4th Amendment. This area gets a lot trickier and a bit more complicated. Do not stop reading here and think you know everything you need about the 4th Amendment or you will certainly find yourself in trouble. As I stated at the outset of this discussion, the police spend the majority of their time working with the 4th Amendment. It contains a lot of gray areas and numerous cases have been won and lost based on either side's understanding of the rights it contains. Again, we have only touched on some basic points. We will get into some of the exceptions to these rules a little later. For now, let move onto the concept of seizures as they apply to the 4th Amendment.

Taking a deeper look into the aspects of what constitutes a "seizure", let's say you are driving down the road and the police pull you over. Is this a seizure under the 4th Amendment?

You have to ask yourself a basic question: Are you free to leave? If the answer is No, then it is a seizure under the 4th Amendment. We all know what would happen if you failed to stop when the police try to pull you over. A "car chase" would ensue and your basic traffic violation will have just turned into a felony.

So, the answer is "Yes", a traffic stop is considered a seizure under the 4th Amendment. A seizure is not just the taking possession of your property, but also removing your ability to move about freely, a seizure of you in your person.

Take another example, you are walking down the sidewalk, minding your own business. A police officer approaches and asks if he or she can speak with you. Can you ignore the officer and keep walking

Unless the officer tells you to stop, they have **asked** to speak with you and you are under no obligation to stop and speak with them. This is an example of a basic street encounter with law enforcement. Now, if the officer tells you to stop or directs you to come to him or her then one could argue that you have been given a lawful order and must comply.

Again, the question courts have asked in these cases is, "are you free to leave?" If the answer is "No", then it is a seizure under the 4th Amendment. When a police officer **directs** you to do something, you must comply. You do not reasonably have a choice. Therefore, you have been seized in your person.

Let me give one last example in this area to test your understanding of this first part of the 4th Amendment before we move on. Let's say you are walking down the sidewalk with a red plastic cup in your hand. You encounter a police officer who suspects your cup contains an alcoholic beverage, illegal under most open container laws. The officer asks what is in your cup. You tell the officer orange juice and keep walking. Have your 4th Amendment rights been violated?

Let's add another spin to this example. What if the officer, while asking you what is in your cup, leans over to smell for alcoholic beverage. Have your 4th Amendment rights been violated?

What if the officer, takes the cup from you to smell for alcoholic beverage, have your 4th Amendment rights been violated?

In the first part of our example, your 4th Amendment rights have not been violated. The police can ask you anything they want during a normal street encounter, traffic stop, etc. On a traffic stop, police often ask all kinds of questions such as: Where are you going?; Where are you coming from?; Where do you work?; Do you have anything illegal in the car? You have the right to answer or not.

I have had friends ask why it is any of the officer's business where they were or where they are going. The answer is that it generally isn't any of their business, but they can ask you anything they want. Whether you choose to answer the question is up to you. I would suggest answering so as not to appear rude and draw more undue attention, but what you say is entirely up to you. In our example with the red plastic cup, nothing says that you have to tell the police what is actually in your cup (we will discuss this later under the 5th Amendment).

In the second part, the same facts from the first part hold true. However, an argument could be made that an illegal search occurred as the officer leaned in to smell the contents of your cup. Now this will definitely lead to arguments on both sides as the officer would say that you did not have an expectation of privacy from the odors emanating from your cup. You on the other hand could argue that the officer's actions went beyond normal observation and became a search when he leaned into your personal space in order to search for odor of alcoholic beverage. While this second part does not have a clear resolution, it should make you think a little as to how both sides can view and argue their point.

In the third part, your 4th Amendment rights have certainly been violated as the officer has seized your property when he took the cup from your possession to search for the odor of alcoholic beverage.

I know your head is probably spinning a little and I know that you probably have a lot of questions, but for now let's keep moving along through the 4th

Amendment as it is written. We will get into the various exceptions and gray areas that will hopefully shed some light on the issues that may be making your head hurt.

Moving onto the second part of the 4th Amendment, we start to get into the whole concept of warrants and probable cause. First, let's take a look at what it says:

> "...no warrants shall issue, but upon probable cause, supported by oath or affirmation..."

The framers of the Constitution were very big believers in the idea that no search or seizure of a person, their property, or their possessions should be allowed without a written warrant or the authorization of a judge. For the most part, this still holds true. However, we do not live in the simple times of the framers and things today have exceptions to this warrant requirement. We will discuss these exceptions and the reasons for them later on. For now, let's just keep this as simple as possible so that we may get a basic understanding of your 4th Amendment protections.

Probable Cause is the idea that more likely than not something is true. It is not an absolute truth as that is for a court to decide during a trial. Rather, an officer seeking a warrant must only show evidence enough to support the fact that a crime, more likely than not, is being or has been committed. From this point, a judge will issue a search or an arrest warrant that the officer can execute.

This does not mean that the judge has already found you guilty of a crime. Rather, the judge has only determined that enough evidence exists that a search be conducted to gather more evidence or that you be arrested and your case be brought to a trial to determine your actual guilt or innocence. Fairly straight forward, right?

Let's move on to the last part of the 4th Amendment which builds upon the concept of a warrant being required for the police to conduct a search or an arrest. It says:

> "…particularly describing the place to be searched, and the persons or things to be seized."

This is pretty self-explanatory, but it requires officers to be extremely specific in their request for a warrant so as to avoid a wrongful search or arrest of an innocent person. For a judge to approve a warrant, it must describe the place or thing to be searched and the person or thing to be seized to the smallest reasonable detail.

For example, a search warrant for a house must describe the physical location of the house such as being located on the northwest corner of Oak and Main Streets, it's numerical house number, the color of the house, the color of any trim work, which way the door to the main entrance faces, whether it has a porch, etc, etc. The way it was explained to me many years ago, was that anyone should be able to locate the correct house even if they have never been to the area before.

The same applies to a person. The warrant should give the person's full legal name, any known aliases, specific physical features such as hair and eye color, height and weight, or markings such as birthmarks, scars, or tattoos. In addition, the person's date of birth, their social security number, their driver's license State and number should be provided. All of this is done to reasonably eliminate the possibility of an innocent person being arrested.

Then, the body of the warrant must contain the specific reasons that establish the "Probable Cause" for the warrant to be issued. If all of this is done correctly, the chances of a wrong place being searched or the wrong person being arrested can be significantly reduced.

That was the goal of the Constitution's framers. They preferred to error on the side of caution rather than infringe upon the rights of the innocent. Not a bad concept. What you must understand is that the legal system was designed to favor the accused. The police and the prosecution have a significant burden to meet in order to make an arrest, much less obtain a conviction. By understanding the system and your rights, you have a much better chance for success in your case.

Now that we have covered the basic concepts and protections guaranteed by the 4th Amendment, let's look at some of the exceptions and muddy the water a little as if it weren't cloudy already.

Warrantless Searches

While obtaining a warrant is always the best way of doing business, the courts have also recognized that under certain circumstances this is not always practical. For example, a police officer walks up to the driver's door of a car and directly observes a package of what appears to be marijuana sitting in "plain view" in the vehicle's center console. In addition, the officer smells what is readily identifiable as marijuana smoke emanating from inside the vehicle. If the officer took this information to a judge to obtain a search warrant, he would most likely be successful. However, when the officer returned, what are the chances the vehicle much less the marijuana would still be present? Not likely.

In cases like this, the courts have ruled that the officer may conduct a search without a warrant due the presence of sufficient probable cause and the likelihood of the evidence's destruction or removal from the scene before a warrant could be obtained.

This sounds fairly reasonable. However, this places a great deal of weight on the officer's judgment rather than the black and white rule of the 4th

Amendment. This is where cases are argued, the gray area of situational judgment. Let's look at another example.

An officer comes to your home to address a complaint of your music being played too loudly. When you open the door, the officer observes various drug paraphernalia and what appears to be marijuana sitting in "plain view" on your coffee table. Under the same principle as the example with the car, the officer may enter your home and seize the illegal drugs.

While this still sounds reasonable, please understand that entire books have been written concerning the 4th Amendment and the use of an officer's situational judgment to make warrantless searches. Not to mention the fact that numerous cases have been lost due to evidence being suppressed after the warrantless search was determined by a judge to have been unreasonable.

I am not by any means attempting to give a complete course on 4th Amendment law, but rather to provide you with some basic understanding and to make you think a little about how the system works so that you can be better prepared to defend yourself in a legal battle.

Warrantless Arrests

Just like in the case of a warrantless search, in a numerous instances, the courts have recognized that it is not practical for an officer to go and obtain an arrest warrant due to the high probability of the suspect disappearing by the time the officer has obtained the warrant.

For example, an officer observes one person physically strike another in some kind of physical altercation. This is obviously an assault by anyone's reasonable standards, reasons for the assault set aside. If the officer left the scene to see a judge and obtain an arrest warrant, what are the chances that the aggressor will be located when the officer returns to the scene? Not very likely.

Therefore, given the circumstances present at the scene and evidence directly obtained by the officer, the courts have recognized the need to make an immediate warrantless arrest.

In another example, let's say an officer stops a drunk driver. If the officer had to leave the scene to find a judge and obtain an arrest warrant, what are the chances that the drunk driver will still be there when the officer returns?

Again, not very likely. Worse yet, the drunk driver probably got back into his car and continued to drive to their original destination, still intoxicated and still a hazard to everyone else on the road. Not a very practical answer for anyone.

Therefore, the courts have again recognized the necessity of warrantless arrests given enough probable cause exists. Numerous violations of the law are treated this way: petit larceny, disorderly conduct, prostitution, minor assaults, domestic violence, etc. While an arrest warrant is always the best way because the probable cause for the arrest has already been reviewed by a judge, it is just not practical in a lot of situations. However, in the case of larger crimes such as those at the felony level, a warrant is almost always issued. This doesn't mean the officer doesn't make the arrest at the time. They do. However, they have a limited amount of time to serve the charging documents on the suspect in the form of an arrest warrant or the suspect is released.

Reasonable Suspicion

Reasonable Suspicion is a step below probable cause. It is not enough in and of itself to substantiate an arrest. However, it is like a building block to get to probable cause. Remember, we defined Probable Cause as the reasonable belief that a crime is being or has been committed. Reasonable Suspicion is such that an ordinary person would suspect that criminal activity has or is about to occur, yet falling short of probable cause to make an arrest. Though it is not enough for an officer to make an arrest or obtain a warrant, it does allow the officer to investigate the activity in order to determine if probable cause exists in order to take further action.

For example, an officer observes a young woman standing on a street corner. The young woman doesn't seem to be going anywhere and she is just hanging around. As cars drive up and stop at the intersection, she casually gestures to them as if looking for a ride. On occasion, a car stops and she walks to the window and has a brief conversation with the vehicle's driver. Several cars pull up and leave after this brief conversation, but the young woman remains standing on the corner. Based on his observations, the officer has developed reasonable suspicion that the woman is a prostitute and is soliciting the drivers of the passing cars. As the officer continues to watch, another vehicle stops. As before the young woman walks to the car's window and has a brief conversation with the vehicle's driver. This time, she gets into the car and it drives away. The officer follows the vehicle and observes it pull down into an alley and park. This would be the next building block in the officer's reasonable suspicion.

We still do not know that this is a case of prostitution, even though it appears to be, thus an arrest is not warranted yet. Then, the officer drives up behind the car and gets out too investigate. His reasonable suspicion of prostitution gives him the authority to detain both the young woman and the vehicle's driver in order to determine if criminal activity is occurring.

After speaking separately with both the young woman and the vehicle's driver, the latter admits to picking up the young woman for sex. This is the point at which the officer's reasonable suspicion graduates into probable cause. He is now justified in making an arrest. Does this make sense?

Prior to the stop and the interview, the officer only possessed the reasonable suspicion of the criminal activity that was occurring. However, the reasonable suspicion is what allowed him to make the "investigative detention" in order to determine if probable cause existed to make the arrest.

I don't know how many times I have had a community member tell me that they believed one of their neighbors was dealing drugs or was involved in some other type of criminal activity. In many of these cases, I believed this this to be true as well. However, it only amounts to reasonable suspicion until enough evidence is gathered to rise to the level of probable cause in order to make an arrest. Sometimes it gets very frustrating, because what you may know and what you can prove are very different things.

Yet, the reasonable suspicion does give me the right to take a closer look at the person and openly investigate them to see if our suspicions are correct. Sometimes they are and sometimes they are not. That is why suspicion alone is not enough for an arrest.

I am sure we have all seen an incident on television or in the movies where a neighbor calls the police because he hears a woman screaming loudly from the apartment next door. Worried, the neighbor believes the woman is being assaulted or worse, killed. The police arrive on scene and hear the same screams. When the police knock loudly at the door and no one answers, they force their way in, reasonably believing that someone's life is in jeopardy. Once inside, they find the man and woman engaged in very aggressive and very loud boisterous sex. No assault is occurring. Talk about an awkward situation, but it happens. Things are not always as they appear and what we suspect to be true may not always be the case.

But, let me ask you this: Were the officers justified in entering the apartment? Sure they were. What if the neighbor's and their suspicions were correct? They may have just prevented a murder or a rape.

Let me give you another example. An officer observes a car in front of him that is weaving in and out of their lane. It's 2:30 am on a Friday morning and most bars have just closed for the night. Based on the circumstances, it is reasonable for the officer to suspect the vehicle's driver is intoxicated.

The officer activates his dashboard camera to capture the evidence of the erratic driving as he continues to follow behind the weaving car. Given the time of night and the manner in which the vehicle is being driven, the officer has established enough reasonable suspicion to stop the car and investigate the situation further.

When the officer reaches the vehicle, he engages the driver in conversation. He observes that the driver's speech is not slurred, he doesn't smell the odor of alcoholic beverage, and the driver explains the weaving as being caused by a dropped lit cigarette. Checking further, the officer asks the driver to exit the vehicle.

The driver complies and exits the vehicle steady on his feet without any indication of intoxication. In addition, as the driver exits, the officer observes a partially crushed cigarette on the seat with an obviously fresh burn mark. At this point does has the officer established probable cause for an arrest?

No, he has not. In fact, the investigation proved that his reasonable suspicion was incorrect and the driver was not intoxicated. Yet, it was the officer's reasonable suspicion that allowed him to make the stop and conduct the investigation. Does this make sense?

The courts allow officers to investigate the possibility of criminal activity based on the reasonable suspicion that such activity has or is about to occur. Otherwise, police officers would never be able to investigate and prevent crime, being relegated to only addressing issues after they had already occurred. In the case of a drunk driver, maybe only after they have crashed into someone and killed them. This is not an acceptable way to protect society.

Though the courts allow officers to temporarily detain people for the purpose of investigating criminal activity, their suspicion alone does not rise to the level of the probable cause necessary to make an actual arrest. They must build upon that suspicion until they either have the probable cause or they do not.

Taking the previous example again, what if when the officer initially speaks to the driver he smells a strong odor of alcoholic beverage emanating from inside the vehicle? Does this establish probable cause?

Not yet. It goes to support the officer's reasonable suspicion that the driver is intoxicated. However, the smell of alcoholic beverage can be explained any number of ways. For instance, the driver admits to just leaving a club and tells the officer he is a bartender, saying he has had numerous alcoholic beverages spilled on him during the course of the night. Sounds like a reasonable explanation.

The officer continues to investigate and observes that the driver's speech is somewhat slurred. Is this enough to establish probable cause to make an arrest?

Maybe, but not yet. What if the driver has a natural speech impediment? The officer continues to investigate, building his reasonable suspicion in order to reach probable cause. He asks the driver to exit the vehicle. As the driver complies, he awkwardly stands up and appears to sway slightly from side to side. Is this enough to make an arrest?

With everything combined, probably. Yet, a good officer will continue to establish more evidence to support his probable cause and have the driver perform several tests, commonly referred to as field sobriety tests.

These tests are designed to force the brain to perform different tasks simultaneously. The alphabet test is probably the most well-known. The driver is required to stand with his feet together or in a heel to toe position and recite the alphabet from a specific starting point and stop at a specific ending point. This is effective because it requires the driver to think about the task at hand, identify the starting point, recite the correct alphabet, and stop at the designated ending point. Simultaneously, the driver must concentrate on maintaining their balance and not fall over. For an intoxicated person, this is a very hard task for the brain to accomplish as it divides its attention between these mental and physical tasks.

As the driver attempts to perform the test, the officer observes slurred speech, an inability to start and stop at the designated places in the alphabet, complete letters are missed in his recitation of the alphabet, and the driver had to reposition his feet several times to prevent falling over. Has the officer established probable cause to make an arrest?

Absolutely, and then some. I have seen officers make arrests earlier in the process and while this is not necessarily wrong, it is always better to obtain as much evidence as you can to have the highest level of probable cause possible.

Either way, do you see how this process works? The officer's reasonable suspicion is the basis for the original stop. As he investigated the situation, his reasonable suspicion grew until he reached the level of probable cause to make the arrest. I hope this explains the difference between reasonable suspicion and probable cause and also provides you with an understanding of how police perform their jobs and what tools they utilize to conduct their investigations. Let's move on.

A Reasonable Expectation of Privacy

The subject of a person's reasonable expectation of privacy relates almost exclusively to searches. We all value our privacy and stand firm to protect ourselves against intrusions. Yet, your privacy has limitations like everything else. A standard of reasonableness is applied to determine whether you could expect your privacy to be maintained or not. To explain this, let's first examine private property versus public property.

If you live in a house, it is obviously your property. However, the land immediately surrounding your home is considered your property as well. In legal terms, it is referred to as "Curtilage". What makes this significant is that the police cannot walk onto your property and spy through your windows in order to obtain evidence. Compare that with an apartment complex. The hallway outside your apartment is common area that is accessible to the public. In many cases, the only thing that you have control over in an apartment type of setting is the apartment's interior. So, the police can literally walk right up to your door.

With a house, the police are required to have a lawful reason for their presence on your property. Thus, in a house you have a greater expectation of privacy than you would in an apartment. Let me give you a couple of examples that should hopefully clarify this.

Working drug cases in particular, a person's trash can yield a great deal of evidence. Therefore, obtaining a person's trash is a great tool. Living in a house, most people have a trash container inside their garage or located just outside next to the home's exterior. Located here, the trash is off limits to the police. Even though it is trash, it is still the person's property because it is located within their curtilage. When trash pick-up day rolls around and the person places their trash at the curb, though it is located on the line of their curtilage, they no longer enjoy the expectation of privacy they had when it was located next to their house.

Simply stated, anyone walking down the street could dig through that trash as it sits alongside of the road waiting for pickup. The homeowner has essentially relinquished their control of it. Therefore, the police are allowed to pick it up as well. Does this make sense?

Compare that to an apartment. In most situations, a person living in an apartment disposes of their trash in a community dumpster. Obviously by the name alone, "community dumpster", the person has relinquished control over their trash and anyone is free to go through it.

Let's say that the person in the apartment sets their trash just outside their front door. Is this public or private? Can the police take this trash?

Absolutely. In most cases, the area just outside the apartment's front door is a common area accessed and used by other members of the apartment complex. Therefore, the person in the apartment has relinquished their control of the trash and their expectation of privacy over it.

Let's look at another example. As the police walk down the hallway of an apartment complex, they observe through a kitchen window various drug paraphernalia and illegal drugs sitting on the counter. Can they enter that apartment and seize those items? Yes they can.

Take the same example but in a house. The police believe that drugs are being sold from inside the home. To gather additional evidence, they walk onto the property and look through a window into the living room, observing the same drug paraphernalia and illegal drugs. Can they enter the house and seize those items? They better not.

In addition, a smart judge will not even grant them a warrant because of the way the information was obtained. The expectation of privacy is different in these two cases. The house is protected by curtilage where the apartment usually is not.

I am going to put another spin on this. Let's suppose the police believe that drugs are being sold out of a house and they park outside on the street to observe any activity at the location. While conducting their surveillance, they use binoculars to look into the house through a window and observe the same evidence as before. Can they enter the house and seize the items?

Yes, though I would strongly recommend obtaining a warrant which a judge would sign without any issue.

This is still a house, right? What about the expectation of privacy? Well, the courts have found that officers may use any of their natural senses and tools that can enhance those senses, such as binoculars, in order to obtain evidence of a crime without violating the curtilage or a person's expectation of privacy. So, in this case, the police are fine.

In larger cases involving the cultivation of marijuana, law enforcement routinely utilize aircraft to fly over areas and look for evidence with thermal cameras, binoculars, etc. Courts have found that this is perfectly legal as the airspace above a property is considered public domain and the use of tools to enhance the natural senses is permitted.

While we are still on the subject of apartments, does a landlord have the right to grant the police access to your apartment? After all, they do own the property right? The answer is "No". For the period of time that you are renting that space, you are the de facto owner. There are very few exceptions where a landlord is allowed to enter your apartment without your permission and the suspicion of criminal activity is not one of them. This same idea applies to a hotel room. The hotel personnel do not have the right to allow the police or anyone entry into your room. You might ask, what about housekeeping? Well, that is with your permission. You have the right to refuse housekeeping services if you choose. That room is your home for the period of time that you are renting it. As such, you enjoy the same right to privacy as if you were sitting in your own personal residence.

Let's look at some more practical day to day examples of expectations of privacy. Courts have found that you have a significantly reduced expectation of privacy with regard to your vehicle.

For example, you park your car at a local grocery store. Though the police cannot necessarily enter your car and search it, they can look through its windows at any items located in its interior. The reason for this is simple: your vehicle is parked in a public parking lot. Anyone walking by can look inside through its windows.

Now, take this same example but the vehicle is parked in the driveway at your home. In this instance, "No", the police are not allowed to examine your vehicle because it is located on your property and protected by your curtilage. In your driveway, you have a greater expectation of privacy.

Take this example to the apartment scenario and the answer is "Yes". Most likely your vehicle is parked in a semi public parking lot, even if you enjoy a designated parking space. Other members of the community can freely walk by your car and have the opportunity to look inside through its windows. You do not have exclusive control over that parking area and therefore have a lesser expectation of privacy. Does this make sense?

I have had people argue with me about my running their license plate and citing them for it being expired. They argue that I don't have the right to check their license plate as it is a violation of their privacy. While I find this argument sort of humorous, I have explained that in the first place their vehicle's license plate is actually property of the state and second it is displayed for the public to view and see. Therefore, it is not even close to being a privacy issue.

In a similar situation, I had someone complain that I was examining the VIN on their vehicle. For those of you not familiar with this, the VIN is the vehicle's serial number imprinted on a thin metal plate located on the dashboard at the driver's side of the car. Again, this is not a violation of anyone's privacy so long as it is being examined in a public place. The VIN is there as a public identifier for that particular vehicle. In fact, it is against the law in most jurisdictions to cover, remove, or alter that VIN plate. It is there specifically to be viewed by police or anyone with a lawful need for that information.

I worked for a number of years as a member of a motorcycle theft unit, attempting to locate and recover stolen motorcycles. We would scour parking lots that had large numbers of motorcycles, examining the VINs.

Despite the strange looks from people and the occasional complaint, this is perfectly legal and outside a person's expectation of privacy.

Another interesting example that has generated the occasional complaint regards the use of drug K-9s. A drug K-9 is called in to search for the presence of illegal drugs through the detection of the drug's odor. This tool is employed in any number of circumstances, but most notably with vehicles.

People have tried to argue that the K-9 smelling around the exterior of their vehicle is a violation of their expectation of privacy. In fact, this issue has yielded some interesting case law.

While the courts have found that though a person has a lowered expectation of privacy concerning their vehicles, an outright search of it cannot be conducted in the absence of probable cause, consent, a search warrant, or a couple of other limited exceptions.

However, as a K-9 smells the air around the exterior of a vehicle, the courts have found that no expectation of privacy exists in the air or odors emanating from inside a vehicle to the outside. Thus, a K-9 "sniff" of a vehicle's exterior is perfectly legal and not a violation of a person's privacy. In addition, a positive alert to the presence of illegal drugs by virtue of the odor emanating from the vehicle is probable cause in and of itself for a full blown search.

Drug K-9s have also been used in cases involving apartments. In these cases, the dog is walked past several doors, including the one suspected of criminal activity. If the dog positively alerts to the presence of odor from illegal drugs, officers are allowed to enter and secure the premise pending a search warrant.

Notice the difference though between the vehicle and the apartment. In the case of the vehicle, a search is permitted on the K-9's positive alert. With the apartment, a search warrant is still required. Officers can enter the apartment to secure it and prevent the destruction of evidence, but a search still requires a warrant. Also, in the case of the apartment, the K-9 is walked past several doors in order to use it as a control to illuminate the possibility of the odor emanating from another apartment.

The reason the officers may search a car that a K-9 has positively alerted to is based on the vehicle's ability to leave the scene with the evidence. In the case of an apartment, it is not going anywhere. I am jumping ahead a little, but I want you to understand the role of K-9s in police investigations and how it relates to your expectation of privacy.

You need to pay special attention to the news and recent events regarding your expectation of privacy. With ever changing technology, the government is attempting to broaden its reach and limit your expectations of privacy in areas such as email, internet search engines, social media sites, and other electronic communications like text messaging. There is and will certainly continue to be new case law as technology changes and the lines of privacy are reexamined and in some cases redrawn.

Summarizing the 4th Amendment

The 4th Amendment is an area that has and will continue to change and evolve over time. It presents any number of challenges that are a reflection of our changing lifestyles, our desire to be safe and secure from governmental intrusion, and our need to be safe from crime. Entire books have been written on the subject and most likely will continue to be as things evolve over time.

On almost a daily basis, numerous challenges are made in courtrooms across this country regarding the way evidence is obtained. In some instances the prosecution wins and in other cases the evidence is suppressed and the defense wins. So everything we have discussed here is by no means the end all be all of the 4th Amendment. In fact, we have only scratched the surface of a very complex issue.

Yet, I do believe that we have covered enough to give you a basic understanding of how things work, what your rights are, and some of the tools used by law enforcement to pursue criminal prosecution. The purpose of this book is to provide you with the basic understanding of your rights and the legal process so that you might think about your particular situation and develop strategies to help you win in court. I strongly suggest that you research and read other publications regarding the 4th Amendment. It is really quite interesting and possibly represents one of the grayest areas in the law.

The 5th Amendment

Anyone who has ever watched coverage of a congressional hearing on television or a high end crime drama on television or at the movie theater has probably heard the defendant state the words, "I take the 5th.

The reason that I describe it as "high end" is simply due to the fact that most ordinary people are not versed well enough in the law to utilize the benefit or the protections provided with this amendment. In most instances, the protections of the 5th Amendment are invoked under the direct coaching of a skilled attorney.

However, everyone is equally entitled to these protections whether under the guidance of legal counsel or from your own base of knowledge. Let's take a look at what exactly the 5th Amendment says:

> "No person shall be held to answer for a capital, or otherwise infamous crime, unless on a presentment or indictment of a grand jury, except in cases arising in the land or naval forces, or in the militia, when in actual service in time of war or public danger; nor shall

> any person be subject for the same offense to be twice put in jeopardy of life or limb; nor shall be compelled in any criminal case to be a witness against himself, nor be deprived of life, liberty, or property, without due process of law; nor shall private property be taken for public use, without just compensation."

While we will discuss each part of the 5th Amendment in detail, the most important part for you to really understand is the third section where is says:

> "...nor shall (any person) be compelled in any criminal case to be a witness against himself..."

The fact of the matter is that most people talk themselves in criminal charges or guilty verdicts. In my experience, it seems as though we have an innate part of our human nature to want to tell the truth or at least attempt to prove our innocence. We defend ourselves by explaining our actions.

Shakespeare said it best, "Thou dost protest too loudly." He means that an innocent person only states their innocence once or twice because he is confident in the truth of his innocence. On the other hand, a guilty person will state their innocence repeatedly and in great earnest because they are not confident in their innocence and are trying to convince themselves as much as their audience.

I can't tell you how many times a suspect has freely given me the information I needed to secure their arrest. In defending ourselves, we rationalize our actions to legitimize our conduct. However, no matter how much we rationalize things, it rarely makes it right in the eyes of the law. Simple strategy, keep your mouth shut.

When an officer reads you your rights, the very first part says:

> "You have the right to remain silent. Anything you say, can and will be used against you."

Take full advantage of that right. As the second part says, everything you say will be used against you. Now, there may be times when it suits your needs to tell your side of the story. However, that is rarely in the field or in the interrogation room.

A good police interrogator can direct your conversation to the point that you are saying things that you never would have said or maybe never intended to reveal when you agreed to talk. Police interrogators spend a lot of time talking with people. They go to extensive training courses to learn how to get information from people. Don't fall into the trap.

Remind yourself that no matter what the police tell you, they are not your friend when you are being interrogated. They have a job to do, namely to secure an arrest and a conviction. The only people truly on your side are your attorney and you.

I know, what about your family? Well, I would suggest caution in that notion as well. Nothing prevents a family member from giving a sworn statement as to their conversation with you. There are exceptions for spouses, but that only extends to the prosecution forcing one spouse to testify against the other. Yet, nothing exists that can prevent a spouse from voluntarily testifying against you.

I know, it sounds a little harsh right? I am only telling you how it is. You must make your own decisions as only you will have to live with the consequences.

"Good Cop, Bad Cop"

I expect that everyone is familiar with this. One cop interrogates you with all the fury he can muster and then another cop comes in to save you from the out of control cop and takes over the interrogation. This second cop is pleasant, shows you respect, and seems to genuinely care about you. This is all a part of the game to get you to lower your guard.

It is a technique designed to get you to view the "good cop" as an ally or a friend. You drop your guard and the next thing you know you are talking your head off. Sound stupid? Maybe, but it works. I have used it. But remember, it is all staged. Who is really on your side? You and your attorney. What is the officer's job? To secure an arrest and a conviction.

Another technique is where an officer tells you that he can see why you did what you did. That he might have done the same thing in your situation. He has been there too. This is all designed to get you to lower your guard and see the officer as a friend or someone who can empathize with you.

Believe me, they are not your friend and are only looking to solidify their case against you. Always remember what their job is. Remember who is really on your side.

In other situations, an officer may ask for your cooperation in other investigations in exchange for recommendations or reductions on your charge. This often entails your making statements about another person that could also be used against you.

Having worked a number of years on narcotics related cases, this is a technique we used frequently. Now, my team and I were on the up and up, meaning that if we promised assistance with bail or sentencing recommendations in exchange for information related to other cases, we made every effort to see it through. It added to our credibility on the street as being fair and "straight" with people. However, not all officers hold to this.

Therefore, I recommend that any deal being proposed to you in exchange for your cooperation or statement be reviewed by your attorney before you say anything. If the deal was good then, it will still be good after your attorney looks it over. Remember, you can rarely take your words back. Once you have said it, it is out there.

It would seem that I have spent a lot of time talking only about police interviews. The same rules apply in a courtroom. You are not required to testify or tell your side of the story. If you defend yourself properly and ask the right questions, you should rarely ever need to actually give testimony.

Another thing to consider when testifying in court, once you tell your side of the story you open yourself up to cross examination by the prosecution, meaning that they can now question you in open court about the statements you just made, statements you made to police, etc. If you do not testify, the prosecution doesn't get the chance to question you. They have to stand on their evidence.

If you think the police can be tough in an interview, try being cross examined by an attorney. This is their job. They can get you to say almost anything on the stand, turn your words around, and having you look like you don't even know your own name. They use some of the same tactics used by the police. One may try to act like your friend. Another may come at you hard. It all depends on their strategy and believe me they have developed a strategy. If you have an attorney, trust them because they are the only one working for you.

Field Sobriety Tests

One last thing to consider before we delve into the other protections contained in the 5th Amendment, field sobriety tests are a form of interrogation. If you are stopped while driving a car after you have been drinking, you do not have to submit to a field sobriety test, breath-a-lyzer, etc. The evidence obtained from these tests will be used against you in court.

Under the 5th Amendment, you cannot be forced to submit to any of these tests and I would strongly recommend that you do not.

You also need to understand that driving under the influence is a unique situation. While you cannot be forced to submit to any tests that can be used against you in a criminal proceeding, your right to drive is a privilege granted to you by the state. As such, when you accept the privilege of driving, you also give your implied consent to submit to any sobriety testing.

Now, refusing to take any sobriety tests will most likely result in your license being suspended for a period of time, but this is an administrative suspension. It is a far cry from being a suspension related to a DUI conviction. The only thing I can recommend is that you suck it up and deal with the administrative suspension and focus on avoiding the conviction for DUI which has much longer lasting ramifications.

Besides, most states will allow you the opportunity to receive a restricted driver's license during the time yours is administratively suspended which grants you the right to drive to and from work, the store, and places of general necessity. We go much deeper into the subject of DUI in another book specifically written on that subject. In any case, think of the sobriety tests the same as an interrogation and keep your mouth shut.

The bottom line with this part of the 5th Amendment is to keep your mouth shut. Don't help the police and prosecution make their case against you. They are not on your side despite their tactics and strategies to make you think so. If you are ever in doubt, consult with a lawyer before you make any statements.

Okay, having really torn into the self-incrimination aspect of the 5th Amendment, let's briefly look at the other protections the amendment provides.

> "No person shall be held to answer for a capital, or otherwise infamous crime, unless on a presentment or indictment of a grand jury, except in cases arising in the land or naval forces, or in the militia, when in actual service in time of war or public danger..."

This section refers to a person being sent to trial for a capital offense such as murder, kidnapping, etc without the charge first being presented to a grand jury.

The purpose of a grand jury is to review the facts of the case and determine if it warrants going to trial. This happens only in the cases where the punishment for the crime is extreme such as the death penalty, life imprisonment, etc. It serves as a safeguard against law enforcement or the prosecution sending you to trial for a case where the evidence is very thin, and considering the possible punishments involved, it is a great safeguard to have.

However, the only caveat that exists to this procedure is for those serving in the military during a time of war. Under that circumstance, a person may be sent to trial without a grand jury indictment. The rules under the Uniform Military Code of Justice are completely different than those in the civilian world.

The next part of the 5th Amendment says:

> "...nor shall any person be subject for the same offense to be twice put in jeopardy of life or limb..."

We touched on this briefly in our discussion of the 1st Amendment. This statement simply means that a person cannot be placed on trial for the same offense twice.

However, the tricky part is found in the "Jeopardy" aspect. This means that for this protection of the 5th Amendment to come into play, a person must have been in jeopardy of losing his life, freedom, money, or some other form of judicial punishment that could result from a guilty verdict.

That is where we said to be careful what you say even after you have been dismissed from court. There are a number of ways a trial can end and not all involve "jeopardy" having attached. If you are found "Not Guilty", then it is a pretty safe bet that you have met the requirements in order to have the protection of the 5th Amendment in this regard. Other than that, be careful what you say. Ask your lawyer before you freely talk about your case. Better safe than sorry.

The next section:

> "...nor be deprived of life, liberty, or property, without due process of law..."

is fairly self-explanatory. We have been talking about the criminal justice process all through this book. This is the system through which you can be deprived of your life, your freedom, or your property. While this may seem like a pretty obvious concept, you need to look at the times during which the Constitution and the Bill of Rights were written.

During that time in our history, British soldiers could seize anything they wanted with very little redress in the courts. So, while this may seem pretty basic to us, it is still a valuable protection to have guaranteed in the Constitution.

Even today in some countries, secret government arrest squads go into people's home in the middle of the night, arrest them, and cart them off to prison. They never have a day in court and some are never heard from again. In some countries, the government can exact financial fines for anything they want and the populace has no way of contesting the seizure of their assets. In other 3rd world countries, the police summarily execute people for crimes they are suspected to have committed. As a U.S. citizen, you are protected by the 5th Amendment from this kind of treatment. The government is required to follow a due process of the law in order to take any action against you.

The last section of the 5th Amendment doesn't particularly deal with the criminal justice system, but is more specific to the civil process.

> "...nor shall private property be taken for public use, without just compensation..."

For example, the government cannot come in and take your house without fair compensation. We hear about this in cases of imminent domain. In these situations, the government may seize your house for the public good such as a new road, park, etc.

However, the government is required to pay you the fair market value of your property. This is another protection that while relevant today in specific cases got its start back in the time of British control over the colonies.

During those times, the army could take over your home and allow their soldiers to stay there without any compensation to you. Worse yet, you would actually be thrown out into the street while the soldiers stayed in your home. This is another great protection that might have been more relevant then, but is still useful today.

So, we have dissected the 5th Amendment and discussed the protections it offers. Probably the most important for our purposes in this book is your right against self-incrimination. Remember this and use it to your advantage. You can never be compelled to give testimony against yourself or provide any evidence that can be used against you. The key here is to "Keep Your Mouth Shut".

The 6th Amendment

Though we have spent a great deal of time on the 4th and 5th Amendments, we would be remiss if we didn't take a look at the protections guaranteed under the 6th. Where the previous two amendments had what I will call practical applications for lack of better words, the 6th Amendment provides security in more of the administrative practices of our legal system. Let's take a look at what it says:

> "In all criminal prosecutions, the accused shall enjoy the right to a speedy and public trial, by an impartial jury of the state and district wherein the crime shall have been committed, which district shall have been previously ascertained by law, and to be informed of the nature and cause of the accusation; to be confronted with the witnesses against him; to have compulsory process for obtaining witnesses in his favor, and to have the assistance of counsel for his defense."

The protections provided for by the 6th Amendment seem to be a little more obscure, but they are equally as important as the others. If you read closely, I know that you are familiar with at least the basic ideas behind this amendment. Probably the most obvious is:

> "... to have the assistance of counsel for his defense..."

It is one of the rights given to a suspect at the time of his arrest. We have all heard it in various television and theatrical police dramas,

"You have the right to an attorney. If you cannot afford to hire an attorney, one will be appointed to represent you."

Sound familiar? This guarantee of your right to legal counsel comes from the 6th Amendment. Yet, other protections are also offered under the 6th Amendment, protections you might not be as familiar with.

> "In all criminal prosecutions, the accused shall enjoy the right to a speedy and public trial, by an impartial jury of the state and district wherein the crime shall have been committed, which district shall have been previously ascertained by law…"

Let's break this first part down a little. It starts by guaranteeing you the right to a "speedy and public trial".

Remember, back when the Constitution was drafted, things were significantly different than they are today. A person could be arrested and thrown into a jail to virtually never be heard from again. A guarantee of a trial did not exist, let alone one held in a public forum.

Though things have obviously changed a great deal from those times, you can still see this type of conduct carried out in other countries around the world. Under the laws of our nation, you cannot be thrown in jail and forgotten. You have the guaranteed right to a trial in a public forum. You are protected from closed door trials where the deck is stacked against you. If the prosecution is going to act corruptly in your prosecution, they will have to do it in the light of day and for all to see, a much harder thing to accomplish. I heard an expression once,

> "Injustice cannot exist in the light of day."

It seems to fit here.

In addition, you have the right to a trial by a jury of your peers. Now, this does not mean that your jury will necessarily consist of everyone being from your racial class, your gender, your income class, etc. It means that your jury will be made up of people from the community in which the crime was committed. Maybe this is not exactly what you had in mind, but it is a lot better than being tried by a jury that is handpicked and stacked against you.

On another note, lesser crimes that are tried in a municipal, magistrate, or village court often afford you the option of what is called a Bench Trial. In this situation, the legal arguments are made before a judge and he makes the final determination of guilt or innocence. While this has some advantages, it still never supersedes your right to a trial by jury. That right is always present and is guaranteed under the 6th Amendment. We will discuss this in greater detail later on. Let's move on.

> "...to be informed of the nature and cause of the accusation..."

This part of the 6th Amendment guarantees you the right to know what you are being arrested for.

Believe it or not, you have the right to know this at the time of your arrest. This is designed to prevent the police from arresting you, taking you to jail, and figuring out a charge later. That is not the way the rules of the legal game are played.

If you are being arrested, you have the absolute right under the 6th Amendment to know the reason and the charge at the time you are taken into custody. If the police fail to provide you with that reason, they have violated your 6th Amendment protections.

> "... to be confronted with the witnesses against him..."

You have the right to confront any witnesses who will testify or otherwise make claims against you. While this may seem pretty basic, it can get a little complicated.

There is a rule commonly referred to as the "Hearsay Rule". It simply means that one person may not testify for another. For example, a police officer is not allowed to state what a witness said or claimed. That is considered Hearsay, and it denies you the right to confront and question your accuser, a violation of your 6th Amendment protections.

An officer may only testify to what they learned or experienced firsthand. We will get into this in much greater detail later, but suffice it to say the 6th Amendment guarantees you the right to confront and question your accuser, not a representative of them.

Finally,

> "... to have compulsory process for obtaining witnesses in his favor..."

The prosecution has the power and authority to force a witness to testify through what is called a subpoena.

The framers of our Constitution were very keen to maintain a level playing field for the citizen in matters dealing with the state. Thus, you are entitled to the same power to bring witnesses to the stand in your defense. Not only may you call upon your own witnesses, but you are allowed to call upon and question any witnesses the state puts forward, including the police.

This last statement is extremely important as I have seen case after case lost because a defendant did not take advantage of his right to question the state's witnesses, especially the police. We will discuss this later as we get more into courtroom preparation and strategy.

Miranda

Your Miranda Warnings are commonly known as reading you your rights. I can remember countless instances where a person I arrested cried foul because I did not read them their rights. Well, here is the short of it.

The police are only required to read you your rights before questioning you about a crime. This does not mean asking general information such as your name, your date of birth, your address, etc. This information is general information only. It does not relate to a crime and therefore does not require your rights be read to you. If a police officer has enough evidence of a crime without the need to question you about it, he is not required to read you your rights.

For example, a police officer witnesses a man walk up and punch another man in the face. The police officer can arrest the man who did the punching for assault without the need to read him his rights. The police officer witnessed the crime and does not need to question the man.

In another example, a police officer stops a young man walking down the street in a high drug neighborhood and asks the young man if he has any drugs in his possession. The young man, for whatever reason, voluntarily pulls a bag of marijuana from his pocket and gives it to the police officer. The officer is not required to read the young man his rights as the evidence of the crime is obvious and no questions need to be asked.

Regardless of the situation, if an officer can establish enough probable cause, a term we discussed earlier, he is free to make the arrest without the need to read a person his rights.

Let's take this in the other direction. Looking at our last example of the young man with the illegal drugs, if he were to be questioned by the officer about where he purchased those drugs, the officer needs to read the young man his rights. The reason for this is that anything the young man might say about the purchase of the drugs can further implicate him in the crime he is charged with. In addition, any statements the young man makes about the purchase of the drugs can lead to additional charges. So, under this circumstance, the officer is required to read the young man his rights.

Probably, the easiest way to understand this is to ask yourself if the officer is questioning you to gather more evidence to support his case against you. If he is, then the officer is required to read you your rights. If the officer's case can stand alone without questioning you, then he is not required to read your rights. There is a fancy legal phrase for this concept, and it is called "prima facie". It simply means on its face. If an officer has prima facie evidence of a crime, no questions are required to support the charge, and he is not required to read you your rights.

Look back at our examples, in all three cases, the officer had sufficient prima facie evidence to make the charge without the need for further questioning. Thus, the requirement for your Miranda Warnings to be given does not exist.

Excited Utterance

If you think that because you made a statement about a crime before you were questioned or you were recorded making statements while sitting in the back of a patrol car and you rights were not read to you and that this is a way to beat the system, you would be sadly mistaken.

Case law exists where a person tried to beat the officer to the punch and made statements about his crime before the officer could read him his rights and ask him a single question. The thought was that if the person could make the statement before his rights were read to him, he could later claim that the officer failed to meet the requirement under Miranda. In addressing this, the courts have said that any statements being made voluntarily and without being questioned by the police are admissible as what has been termed "excited utterance".

Take our first example of one man walking up and punching another man in the face. The officer observed the incident and therefore is not required to read the man his rights before placing him under arrest. In addition, at the moment of the arrest, let's suppose the officer asks, "What did you do that for?" The man replies, "Because I found out he was sleeping with my girlfriend." That statement is completely admissible in court. Why you might ask? It was not a formal interrogation. It was a statement made in the heat of the moment and thus is considered an "excited utterance".

While the police have specific rules under which they must operate, they are also not responsible to educate you on each of your guaranteed rights under the Constitution.

With the exception of formal interview and interrogation, it is your responsibility to know your rights and invoke them when necessary to protect yourself. Among your rights, the most important one is the first,

> "you have the right to remain silent."

Use that right. Don't be the idiot that runs around yelling, "they didn't read me my rights." They may not have to and you are demonstrating just how ignorant you are. Know what your rights are and how to use them. Remember, anything you say, can and will be used against you in court. The only people truly on your side are your lawyer and you.

The Hearsay Rule

We might be jumping ahead just a bit, but this was brought up a little earlier in this book. The Hearsay Rule really applies to the courtroom setting. However, I think we ought to discuss it now before we move on. This way, you will see how it works and how you can use it to your advantage when we get into our discussion of courtroom testimony.

Something is considered "Hearsay" if you do not know the information for yourself, firsthand. This means that you cannot say what another person saw, what another person felt, or what another person experienced. Unless they told you something directly, you cannot even say what another person said. If you do, this is called Hearsay and it is inadmissible in court. This is important because it can help in your courtroom defense.

An officer is not allowed to testify on another person's behalf. He cannot say what a victim saw, what they felt, or what they experienced. He cannot recount any statements they might have made during the time of the incident unless the officer was present to hear it for himself firsthand, and even then he must phrase his testimony to reflect that. Believe it or not, this is a lot harder than it sounds.

Let's look back at our first example under our discussion of Miranda, but with a couple of changes. Rather than the officer being present to see the assault take place, he arrives after the fact. All of the evidence points to the one man having assaulted the other. So, he is arrested. When the case comes to court, the victim does not show up, leaving the officer to prosecute the case himself. The officer is not allowed to make statements for the victim. He cannot recount the events that led up to the assault or specifically what happened during the assault itself. He was not there to witness it firsthand. Only the victim can testify to those facts. If the officer tries to testify to those facts in light of the victim's absence in court, this constitutes Hearsay and is inadmissible.

The officer is only allowed to testify to what he has firsthand knowledge of, evidence he observed at the scene, and statements made directly to him by either the victim or the defendant. The Hearsay Rule maintains the constitutional protections guaranteed under the 6th Amendment, namely a person's right to confront their accuser.

This one rule alone can cost the prosecution their case and allow you to win in court. Pay attention to what is said, know the rules, and be prepared to raise objections if you feel the officer or the prosecution is stepping out of line. It is the judge's responsibility to make sure the rules are followed. The worse thing that can happen if you raise an objection is that the judge over rules you and allows testimony to continue. Either way, you should never be afraid to object to testimony if you believe it is in violation of the Hearsay Rule.

Amendments Concluded

While we have discussed the most relevant and important protections guaranteed to you in the Constitution as they relate to the criminal justice system, so much more exists out there to explain them even further. We have only touched on them enough to give you a fair understanding of your rights and protections.

Please read more and learn more. These are the rules of the game. The police are expected to follow them and so are you. But, if you don't know the rules, how can you expect to win?

It is your responsibility to know your rights. It is not the job of the police or the prosecution to educate you on them. Our prisons are full of jail house lawyers who learned the law and their rights after they were already in prison. You don't have to wait until then. Learn now. Knowledge is power and those who have it rule.

2

The Process of Arrest

There are several ways in which you can be arrested by the police. I am not talking about reasons the police may have for stopping you, but the ways in which you are actually arrested. Some of them may be obvious, but others may surprise you. We will look into each of them separately to explain and show some of the differences. However, at the end of the day, an arrest is an arrest.

Custodial versus Non-Custodial Arrests

First, we must look at and understand the difference between a custodial and a non-custodial arrest. Their name really says it all. A custodial arrest is when the police actually place handcuffs on and take you to the jailhouse. This is not to say that every time the police place someone in handcuffs they are under arrest. This is not always the case either.

The police have the power to place a person into what is commonly called "investigative detention" which is usually accompanied by the use of handcuffs, but not always. It a tool used by the police to detain a person while they investigate a crime in the field. For example, they may know that they have their suspect but don't have enough to make an immediate charge.

So, the person is detained for a reasonable amount of time in the field while the police attempt to gather enough evidence to make a decision whether to arrest. If they cannot collect enough evidence to reach probable cause, the person is released from investigative detention and is free to go.

Now, under an investigative detention, the police have the power to place a person into handcuffs if they have reason to believe doing so is a matter of safety for themselves, the public, or the person being detained. Let me say it again, a person under investigative detention is not yet under arrest, handcuffs or not.

Investigative detention may simply be not letting you leave the area, or making you sit on the curb, or placing you in the backseat of the patrol car. You also need to keep in mind that under an investigative detention, you are not free to leave.

Think back to our discussion of the 4th Amendment and your protections granted under it. Before we get into that, let's look at another type of investigative detention, a traffic stop for DUI.

An officer observes you driving your vehicle excessively slow with regard to the posted speed limit, one among the many tell-tale signs of a drunk driver. He pulls you over to investigate. At this point, the officer does not have enough evidence to establish probable cause to make an arrest.

Obviously, there are many reasons that can explain the slow driving besides intoxication. Therefore, the officer must investigate further to see if the driver is truly intoxicated. You may consider this an investigative detention.

You have not necessarily broken any laws and you are not under arrest. However, the officer has the power to detain you and you are not free to leave. Now let's look back at our discussion of your protections under the 4th Amendment. Do you see it yet?

By the definitions set forth in the 4th Amendment, under an investigative detention, you have been seized in your person. Though you are not under arrest, neither are you free to leave. As we discussed, the police have the power to detain individuals based on a reasonable suspicion that a crime has been, is being, or is about to be committed. Then, they have to investigate further in order to meet the threshold of probable cause to proceed with an arrest.

In addition, an investigative detention must be reasonable in its length. Now, this is quite a grey area as to what constitutes a reasonable amount of time a person may be detained. I wish I could give you that answer. However, the courts have been reluctant to set hard time limits on investigative detentions because every situation is different. Thus, a court would have to decide if the length of your detention was reasonable based on your particular circumstances.

In any case, I want you to understand that you might find yourself in police custody, but not necessarily under arrest. Also, I want you to relate your protections under the various amendments to the various situations we are going to discuss through the remainder of this book and see how they all come together to create the criminal justice system.

The police and the prosecutors have rules under which they must operate which are the same as the protections you have under the Constitution. This is the whole point of this book. If you know the process and the rules that are designed to protect you, you also know the rules that the police and the prosecution are required to work within. You can't cry foul if you don't know what is out of bounds. Keep this in mind as we move forward.

Ok. Let's take a look at non-custodial arrests. If you understood a custodial arrest, then this should be pretty obvious. However, it also begs the question, how can I be under arrest and not be in police custody?

A traffic ticket is the simplest example. When you are issued a traffic citation, you have been arrested. Most of the time, you are not taken into police custody or transported to jail, but you have been arrested nonetheless.

Think of a speeding ticket. Most of us have gotten at least one of those in our lifetime and yet, few, if any of us, have been taken to jail just for speeding. This is the most common form of non-custodial arrest. However, this is not limited only to traffic violations.

Anytime you are charged with a crime and issued a summons, you have been arrested even though you are not taken to jail. It is commonly referred to as a courtesy summons, the courtesy lay in the fact that you were not taken to jail at the time of your arrest.

In my jurisdiction, our department allowed us to make custodial arrests on any criminal charge or traffic violation. For the most part, it was up to our discretion. However, courtesy summonses had limitations.

For example, simple possession of marijuana was a custodial arrest. Driving without a license or driving with a suspended license was a custodial arrest.

These rules are set by individual departments and vary depending on what part of the country you live in.

For example, some jurisdictions issue a courtesy summons for the simple possession of marijuana. Other jurisdictions, issue a courtesy summons for driving without a license or driving with a suspended license, but tow the vehicle to ensure it is not used by the offender again. It varies depending on the department and the political climate at the time.

I just want you to be clear that an arrest is not always defined as being placed into handcuffs, nor is it always only defined as being taken to jail.

Arrest Warrants

A warrant for your arrest is a document that has been reviewed by a judge to ensure that probable cause exists for you to be placed under arrest and taken to jail. They are not a determination of your guilt or innocence, but rather a review of the probable cause for the arrest.

As a judge has reviewed the case and signed off on it, an arrest warrant is the highest authority in determining the lawfulness of an arrest. It is nothing short of a court order that the arrest be carried out.

While all are approved by a judge and the end result is the same, warrants for your arrest can come in many forms. The most common is a simple arrest warrant. This is where an officer puts a case together, including all of the reports and evidence he has been able to obtain, summarizes it all in the application for the arrest warrant and submits it to a judge for review.

The judge then reviews all of the evidence and the application for the arrest warrant to determine if the officer has met the probable cause threshold. If he has, then the judge approves the warrant for the arrest. On the other hand, if the judge determines that the officer has failed to meet the probable cause burden, then the application is denied and returned to the officer who must then gather additional evidence before reapplying for the warrant.

From an officer's point of view, arrest warrants require a lot more work and certainty to obtain. However, once the judge has approved the arrest warrant, the burden of probable cause has been lifted from the officer's shoulders as the judge has now assumed it through his approval of the warrant.

While it is more time consuming for the police, it is always considered the safest way to make an arrest. A warrantless arrest works more in your favor because it gives you another avenue to argue your case from the point of view of whether probable cause existed to make the arrest. However, just because a judge approved an arrest warrant does not mean that you cannot argue its probable cause. It is just exponentially more difficult.

Another kind of warrant is referred to as a citizen's arrest warrant. This occurs when an everyday citizen seeks to obtain a warrant for your arrest. It is virtually the same as that which might be sought by a police officer. However, the citizen usually only has the report taken by the police officer and then their side of the story. It is then between the citizen and the judge as to whether the warrant is issued.

In my experience, this happens when the officer taking the report doesn't feel that enough evidence exists to make an arrest, but the citizen insists an arrest be made. When it comes time for court, it is the citizen versus the person arrested.

The tricky part of this process is that anyone can seek an arrest warrant for anyone else. It is up to the judge to determine if a warrant shall be issued or not. In your favor is the fact that if the officer didn't feel that probable cause existed to pursue an arrest, the citizen is going to have a difficult time in obtaining the warrant. Does it happen anyway?

Yes, of course it does. Again, the burden of probable cause then falls on the judge. Either way, once an arrest warrant is signed by a judge, it is a court ordered arrest and the police do not have any discretion in carrying it out.

The last basic form of an arrest warrant is when the judge issues the warrant on his own behalf. This is commonly referred to as a Bench Warrant. This kind of warrant is issued when a person fails to appear in court, fails to pay a fine, violates a court order, or in general pisses off the judge.

In our system, judges reign supreme above the criminal justice process in many regards. They can have police officers arrested for contempt of court which usually entails failing to follow a court order. They can have lawyers arrested in their courtroom. They can have people placed under arrest for a cell phone ringing in their courtroom. They are the gods of their universe.

As with any other arrest warrant, Bench Warrants are court ordered arrests. The police do not have any discretion over the process once a warrant has been issued. They are essentially commanded by the court to make the arrest.

Search Warrants

Just like in our discussion of an arrest warrant, a search warrant is always the most preferable way for a police officer to do business. It is a document that outlines in very specific detail the person or place to be searched, the things to be searched for, and the reasons that make the search necessary.

An officer drafts a search warrant and then makes application to a judge to have it issued. The safety in this is the same as that found in an arrest warrant, a judge has previewed the facts of the case and determined a search warrant is necessary to further the investigation.

Just as in the discussion of an arrest warrant, if the judge finds the reasons for the search warrant are not substantial enough or the person or place to be searched is not clear enough, or the items sought in the warrant are not clear enough or relevant to the investigation, he will deny the search warrant, sending officers back to the drawing board to try again.

Just like an arrest, searches do not always have to be done under the issuance of a warrant. That is just the best way because of the judicial review before the action is taken. Several instances exist where an officer may conduct a warrantless search of a person or their property. The most obvious of these is a consensual search.

This is exactly what it sounds like. You may freely give the police permission to search you, your car, your home, or any other property that you own. However, you may not give permission for an officer to search someone else's person or property with maybe one exception, your children.

The key to remember here is that even though you may give a police officer the permission to conduct a search, you may take back that permission at any time and the officer must stop the search immediately. In addition, when you give the police permission to search, you may also limit the scope of that search.

For example, you might give the police permission to search you home, but tell them that your bedroom is off limits and not to be searched. Compare this to an actual court issued search warrant and the rules are totally different. The search warrant gives the police the permission to search anyone and anything within the realm of that warrant.

However, just as if you gave the police limited permission to search you or your property, the police may not search outside the scope of their warrant. For example, if a search warrant is issued to seek stolen televisions in your home, the police may only look where it is reasonable for a television to be. Thus, they cannot look through drawers, kitchen cupboards, in shoeboxes, etc because a television could not fit there. These places would be outside the scope of their warrant.

So, let's say the police are searching your home for stolen televisions and look into a kitchen drawer where they find other illegal items. You cannot be arrested for that because it constitutes an unlawful search when the police violated the scope of their search warrant by looking into the kitchen drawer for a stolen television. If you are arrested, the police have a lot of explaining to do in order to get around their illegal search. Make sense?

When I worked drug cases, the nature of my job made search warrants a lot easier because drugs can be hidden virtually anywhere. Thus, I could look virtually anywhere and any other illegal items I found could be used to make an arrest even if those items were not necessarily drug related. Do you see the difference and understand what we mean by the scope of the search?

Another type of warrantless search exists under what is called exigent or emergency circumstances. This comes into play when there is a strong likelihood of evidence being removed from an area or destroyed before a search warrant could be obtained.

For example, on a traffic stop, a police officer smells the odor of marijuana emanating from inside the vehicle. By the time the officer could get a search warrant, the suspect will have driven away with the marijuana, it might be thrown out of the car onto the ground and destroyed, or the rest of the marijuana might be smoked. So, in this example, exigent circumstance exists and the officer has the right to search the interior of that vehicle and the vehicle's occupants for the marijuana without a search warrant.

Also, consider in this example, the officer cannot search the trunk of the vehicle unless he can reasonably argue that an odor of marijuana was readily and easily recognizable emanating from inside the trunk. While this is possible, it is very unusual.

I have had this happen on one case I worked. The odor of marijuana from the trunk was so strong that when I finally opened it, the smell almost knocked me over. Then again, 60 pounds of marijuana was inside the trunk in poorly sealed freezer bags with nothing else used to mask the odor. But, this is the exception more than the rule.

Moving on, the U.S. Supreme Court has held that an officer may use any of his natural senses to determine the existence of evidence of criminal activity. In addition, an officer may use any piece of equipment that enhances his natural senses to assist in the discovery of this evidence such as binoculars. As long as the officer can articulate the existence of exigent circumstances, he may search without a warrant.

However, as is everything else we have discussed, the exercise of free power comes with a greater amount of scrutiny when the case comes to court. These are the loop holes that you need to see and understand in order to be successful within the criminal justice system. The only way you can do this is by knowing and understanding your rights and the rules by which the legal game is played.

Let's back up for just a second, I want you to look back at the traffic stop and the marijuana example we just discussed. How does this fit with the 4th Amendment? How does it fit with arrest procedures, specifically the concept of an investigative detention?

Where the 4th Amendment is concerned, in the absence of a search warrant, an officer must have probable cause to conduct a warrantless and non-consensual search. His recognition of the marijuana odor emanating from inside the vehicle establishes his probable cause. Again, this something you would want to seriously examine and question in court. The only protected way that a police officer may conduct a search is with a warrant.

Onto the idea of investigative detention, we have already concluded that the police may detain someone for a reasonable amount of time while they investigate a case to determine if probable cause exists for an arrest. I suppose one might argue, why can't the police just detain the driver of the car and get a search warrant?

Well, the short answer is the time it would take to write the warrant and then find a judge to sign off on it would be outside of what anyone would consider reasonable for the driver to be detained along the open roadway. In addition, you still must contend with the issue of the evidence being destroyed before the search warrant can be issued and executed.

There are probably a hundred other reasons and explanations. I am just trying to get you to think and understand how and why things happen the way they do. In understanding these things, it makes you better prepared to defend yourself in court should that day ever come.

Another exemption to the need for a search warrant is called the plain view doctrine. This simply states that if an officer can see evidence of criminal activity in plain sight, he has the power to seize that evidence immediately without a search warrant.

Again, this goes back to the argument of exigent circumstance. Let's say an officer responds to a home on a noise complaint. When the person opens the home's front door, the officer can clearly see a large number of teenagers drinking alcoholic beverages, empty beer cans and bottles strewn about the floor, and some of the teenagers obviously intoxicated. The officer can enter the home to seize the evidence of the alcoholic beverages and make arrests where required. If the officer were to leave and attempt to obtain a search warrant for the home, the party would most likely be over by the time he returned, the alcoholic beverages might have been removed, etc. As the officer saw the evidence of criminal activity in plain view, he has the power to act on it without the need of a search warrant.

Now, for our purposes, we are not trying to describe in detail what an officer may or may not do just for the sake of argument. Again, the point is that you need to understand how things work if you are to defend yourself in court. When an officer uses his discretion and any of the many exceptions to the rule, he leaves himself open to more scrutiny in court.

This is the gray area that you need to exploit in your defense. The police are people and they can make mistakes. The judge and the jury are people who might relate to your side of things. Just understand the process so you can make an argument in your own defense when the time comes.

In addition to the various ways the police may conduct a search, with and without a search warrant, still a couple of more yet remain. These are especially unique tools used by the police to conduct searches without a warrant. Therefore, we are going to highlight each of them separately.

Search Incident to an Arrest

When a person is placed under custodial arrest for any crime, the police have the authority to search their entire person, including all of their clothes and possibly even a full blown strip search depending on the circumstances.

This is allowed for a variety of reasons such as conducting an inventory of your personal belongings, ensuring that you are not concealing any weapons, and attempting to locate additional evidence of criminal activity. In addition to your person, the police may search any of your personal items such as bags, purses, boxes, etc that you may have in your possession at the time of your arrest.

The police are not required to obtain a search warrant for a search conducted on a person after the arrest has been made. The courts have recognized that, in addition to the reasons we have already given, the search of an arrested person is a matter of safety.

Think about this: The police arrest a person for shoplifting and take them to jail without searching them. The person has a gun, a knife, or illegal drugs concealed on their person that are now being brought into a detention center. Even if the arrested person has no intent to use the items, there exists a possibility that another inmate might.

Take the same example, except stop short of actually making it to the jail. The arrested person is placed into the back of the patrol car. He removes a gun that was concealed on his person and shoots the officer dead as they drive to the jail.

Unfortunately, this sort of thing has happened on a number of occasions. If the police officer had searched the prisoner before putting him into the patrol car and taking him to jail, this all could have been avoided. So, while there is obviously an evidentiary reason for the search of a person after they have been arrested, it also safe guards the persons personal items and prevents unnecessary harm coming to others.

While some of you may not be a fan of the police, I am merely trying to explain why they do what they do and what empowers them to do it.

Terry Frisk or Pat Down

This is not a full blown search. Instead, it is exactly what its name says, a "Pat Down". Again, the courts have recognized the safety of the officer, the suspect, and the public as an overriding factor in allowing the police a certain amount of leeway around your 4th Amendment protections. However, as with all exceptions to any rule, strict guidelines are required to make the search valid.

For example, an officer must be able to articulate the reason a "Pat Down" was necessary and it must be such that any reasonable person would agree. The suspect must show some sign of possibly wanting to harm the officer, destroy evidence, or conduct some other action that would cause harm to the officer or the general public. These signs can include acting agitated, overly nervous, shifting of weight from on foot to another, or constantly reaching down to touch a pocket or some other place where a weapon might be concealed. While the reasons can be very subjective, an officer must be able to justify the "Pat Down".

Other rules of a "Pat Down" search prohibit an officer from reaching into your pockets, reaching into your waistband, removing of any items of clothing, and manipulating any items felt in your pockets in order to determine what those items might be.

A "Pat Down" search is conducted of your outer clothing in places where a weapon might be concealed. The "Pat Down" is designed for officer safety and not for the purpose of locating evidence. The manual manipulation of items felt in a person's pockets during a "Pat Down" search is probably among the biggest mistakes the police make in this type of warrantless search.

For example, an officer conducting a "Pat Down" search feels an item in a person's front pants pocket. The officer cannot squeeze, twist, or try to feel the object in attempt to determine what the object might be. If it were a gun, it would be pretty obvious on the "Pat Down" and not require the manipulation. That is the purpose of this type of search.

I have read reports where officers have written that while conducting a "Pat Down" search of a person, they felt what was readily and easily identifiable as a bag of marijuana concealed in the person's front pocket. How is that possible?

First, the officers overstepped the bounds of the "Pat Down" search. Second, readily and easily recognizable? What if it was a plastic bag containing nothing? What if the plastic bag contained oregano or anything besides the marijuana? It is not possible that the officers could know what was in that person's pocket from a "Pat Down" search even if they wrongfully manipulated it in attempt to figure out what it was. It was written right there in their official police report documenting the arrest.

Just think, if that person had known the rules that we are explaining in this book and the protections guaranteed them under the U.S. Constitution, it would have been an easy case to win. The police overstepped their bounds and the evidence was obtained from an illegal search. The evidence would have been suppressed and the case dismissed.

The unfortunate reality is that the person may have only attempted to plea bargain their charge down, if they did anything at all. Understand your rights and understand the process.

Vehicle Inventory

Many officers confuse a vehicle search with a vehicle inventory. The latter is an inventory of the vehicle's contents after its driver has been arrested and before the vehicle is towed to an impound yard. While at the end of the day, one could still argue that it amounts to a search, it is an inventory that may yield the same result as a search.

I know what you are thinking, semantics right? Well, the law is often based strictly on semantics, words have meaning. A search of a vehicle prior to the driver being arrested from that vehicle is a search.

For example, the police may have reason to arrest a passenger from a motor vehicle. As a search incident to the arrest, they can then search the area inside the vehicle where that passenger could have accessed or concealed evidence. This is often referred to as the "wing span rule". Wherever, the passenger could have reached is subject to search. Depending on the size of the vehicle, this may or may not extend to the other areas of the vehicle and it rarely entails a search of the vehicle's trunk.

Now, let's say that the driver was arrested from the vehicle. The same "wing span rule" applies for a search incident to the driver's arrest. It still may or may not include all areas of the vehicle's interior depending on the vehicle's size and again, it would rarely extend to the vehicle's trunk space.

However, as the driver was arrested, it is fairly probable that the vehicle is going to be towed to a police impound yard. As the police are now taking custody of the vehicle, they are charged with the safekeeping of its contents. It's hard to be responsible for something if you don't know what is there. Thus, the police are allowed to conduct a thorough and complete inventory of the entire vehicle prior to it being towed. Wa la, the police now have access to the entire vehicle.

If they find evidence of criminal activity during the inventory, it is chargeable against the driver. Do you see how this works?

Let's say the police stop a suspected drug dealer for failing to use his turn signal. Depending on the jurisdiction, they may be able to arrest him for that simple violation and then search the vehicle under the guise of an inventory prior to the vehicle being towed to the impound yard. It's dirty pool, but legal.

The police bend the rules to meet their needs without going so far as to break them outright. So, dirty pool or knowing how to work within the system?

This is not to say that the police won't be questioned harshly in court about the arrest for a turn signal violation and they may even have to produce documentation that the arrest is a normal course of action for this type of offense in order to avoid a profiling or harassment charge. Yet, their actions are legal.

It is important that you recognize the difference between a search incident to an arrest from a vehicle and a vehicle inventory search. As I said before, it's not that the police did anything wrong, but many confuse the issue. If they can't explain their actions in court, the "why" they did what they did, you have a pretty good chance of prevailing in your case.

Protective Sweeps

This is a very simple concept, so we are not going to spend a lot of time on it. When the police lawfully enter your residence for reasons other than to execute a search warrant, they are entitled to perform what is referred to as a protective sweep of the premise. Essentially, they are allowed to walk through your home and make sure someone isn't hiding inside that could harm them while they are investigating the reason for their being in your home.

For example, the police receive a report of a fight taking place inside your home. When they arrive you answer the door and allow them to come inside. While you explain that no fight had occurred and that you and a friend were watching an action movie on television with the volume turned up too loud, the officer has the right to walk through your home looking for anyone who might do him harm while he is investigating his original call.

This does not mean a police officer can look in drawers, dig through closets, etc. He is only allowed to look in places where a person might hide and that is cursory at best, meaning not looking under every bed and in every closet.

The officer's protective sweep must be reasonable to ensure his personal safety. That is the extent of it.

Now, keep in mind that during his protective sweep of the premise, if that officer finds evidence of criminal activity in plain view, he in entitled to act upon it under the plain view doctrine. See how one thing can lead into another?

The Use of Police K-9

An officer may call for the assistance of a police K-9 whenever they feel it necessary. There aren't any rules that specifically determine when an officer can request that type of assistance or when a police K-9 may be used. Sometimes, a police K-9 unit just shows up on various traffic stops to assist or other times he may be working in tandem with a traffic interdiction team.

When a police K-9 walks around your vehicle, he sniffs the air that seeps between the cracks, the seals, the open windows, or the door. They are specially trained to recognize numerous odors and differentiate them from other odors that might be present. It has been argued in court that this "sniff" of a vehicle's exterior is a violation of the 4th Amendment as it constitutes an illegal search. The courts have maintained that you have a lower expectation of privacy in a vehicle than you would in your home. In addition, the air around a vehicle is public and not specifically owned by anyone. Thus, a police K-9 may sniff the air around a vehicle without it becoming an issue under the 4th Amendment.

While I have worked a great deal with police K-9s and their handlers, I am not one. Therefore, I will have to stay away from specifics that I am really not qualified to get into. However, I will explain the general processes through which a police K-9 is used and their basis for establishing probable cause.

When a police K-9 performs a "sniff" around the vehicle's exterior and detects an odor of illegal drugs, that is enough in and of itself to establish probable cause for an officer to search the car. You may ask why that is all that is required?

The courts have long upheld the accuracy and reliability of a K-9s ability to sniff out drugs, explosives, people etc. They are a very well-known asset with an extensive track record over decades of use.

Now, with that said, an individual K-9's ability may be called into question. The handler is required to maintain detailed training documentation for his dog. In addition, the K-9 is required to complete recertification tests on a regular basis with a fairly high hit rate for accuracy. If the handler cannot produce this documentation, the K-9's reliability can be called into question.

However, this is a pretty steep hill to climb in order to overcome the courts general acceptance of K-9s and their abilities. In some cases, the argument may be worth making, but don't hold your breath or count on it as your primary defense.

In addition to using K-9s for vehicle searches, they have been used successfully in situations involving apartments and hotel rooms. These are obviously different than a motor vehicle and they present unique challenges for the police.

For example, let's say in a hallway with ten hotel rooms numbered 101 – 110, room number 105 is suspected of containing illegal drugs. While it would be easy to just walk the K-9 up to that door and sniff for the odor of illegal drugs, it will just not suffice in court. Instead, the handler must walk the K-9 past several rooms before and after the suspect room to serve as a "control".

The fact that the K-9 does not alert to the rooms before or after the suspect room, but does alert to the suspect room itself is where the case is made.

Now, this does not work in all situations. The problem is the police officer's lawful presence. For example, the police cannot just walk a K-9 up to the front door of your house and sniff for illegal drugs. Do you remember the "Curtilage" aspect of your property and your right to privacy that we discussed earlier?

This is the reason the police cannot use this tactic on your home. Even in some apartment or hotel situations, the same "Curtilage" rules may apply. The situation must be such that the area immediately outside of the apartment or hotel room's door is open to the public, such as in the case of a hallway used by other residents to reach their doors. This public nature of the hallway is what allows the police to walk the K-9 up to your door for the sniff.

Take as an example an apartment where there exists a hallway that is shared by other residents to reach their residence. However, off from this main hallway is another short passage that leads to your front door. How does this play into the idea of curtilage?

Well, it would certainly be an interesting situation and certainly the argument can be made, the grounds for which are based on the idea that while the common walkway is shared by all the residents, the portion leading up to your specific door is unique to your property. Curtilage may apply.

Again, I am not a judge or a lawyer. I am just attempting to get you to see and think about how it all comes together in different situations.

So, take our example of the hotel room, the police K-9 sniffs at several doors before and after the suspect room, but alerts only to an odor coming from inside the room in question. This is not enough to allow the police a full blown search of the hotel room as was the case with a motor vehicle. Instead, the positive alert allows the police to enter the room, secure it, and detain its occupants while a search warrant is obtained. The only reason the police are even allowed to enter the hotel room is due to the exigent circumstances that we discussed earlier. Now, if there are illegal drugs laid out in plain view when the police enter the room, they are fair game. The police are just prohibited from conducting any actual search for the items. Make sense?

We have spent a great deal of time discussing how police K-9s are often utilized. Let's look at couple of situations where they are often prohibited from being used.

For example, police K-9s are rarely if ever used to detect illegal narcotics on a person. Officers may bluff this and say that the dog is going to check you, but it is rarely ever allowed. The reasons are fairly obvious. Though police

K-9s are highly trained animals, they are still animals with a certain amount of unpredictability. The last thing any department wants is to have their police K-9 checking a person when it decides to bite. Can we say major lawsuit?

In addition to that, some police K-9s are trained to passively alert to the presence of illegal drugs by sitting down. Other police K-9s are trained to alert actively by biting or digging at the area where they detected the odor of illegal drugs. Police departments certainly do not want their active alert police K-9 detecting the odor of illegal drugs on a person.

Other things to Consider

We have discussed arrest procedures and arrest warrants. We have also discussed the many ways the police may lawfully conduct a search with and without a warrant. I just want to touch on a couple more things before we move onto the courtroom procedure section of this book.

Constructive Possession

I can't think of how many times more than one person has been charged with the crime of a single individual. Doesn't sound fair does it? Well, the principle we call Constructive Possession is similar to the concept

"hand of one is the hand of all".

Probably the easiest way to explain this is to just give you an example.

Say you are driving down the road in your car with a couple of your friends and you get stopped by the police for some type of minor traffic violation. One of your friends in the backseat gets nervous, takes a bag of marijuana out of his pocket, and hides it between the two front seats. You had no idea that your friend had marijuana in his possession, much less that he has now hidden it in your car.

During the course of the traffic stop, the police officer asks you for consent to search your vehicle for illegal drugs. The whole thing for the officer is fairly routine, and to your knowledge there aren't any illegal drugs in your vehicle, so you give your consent for the search.

As the officer searches your vehicle, he locates the bag of marijuana stuck down between the two front seats. You are shocked, protesting that you do not use drugs and that you have no idea where the marijuana came from. Your friends also deny knowing anything about the marijuana that has now been found in your car. The officer is left with very little option, but to take everyone to jail for the marijuana.

He can't prove whose it was and everyone in the vehicle had equal access to it from its location between the two front seats. Therefore, everyone was in constructive possession of the marijuana and everyone is charged. Doesn't sound fair does it?

The fact is that the marijuana was in your car. No one claimed it. You all had equal access to it and just as equal an opportunity to hide it between the seats. The marijuana can't just disappear and the officer needs to charge someone for it. If he can't prove who the marijuana belongs to, the officer is well within his authority to charge everyone.

Another way to explain this is one that I have used numerous times out in the field. I stand there with a person and I hold a pen in my hand. At that moment, I am in sole possession of the pen. Then, I lay the pen on the ground equal distance between us. At that moment we are both in constructive possession of the pen. We both have equal access and opportunity to the pen.

One last example: It's sort of a sad case. We surveilled a suspect believed to be in selling moderately sized amounts of crack cocaine. He was picked up by a female and driven from the area. We elected to perform a traffic stop on the vehicle hoping the suspect would have the crack cocaine on him so an arrest could be made.

When we stopped the vehicle, we found it occupied by a female driver, the suspect, and a 6 month old infant. The child was that of both the driver and the suspect. However, the driver and the suspect were only in a casual relationship.

Obviously working an illegal drug case, we had a police K-9 handler standing by. He responded to the scene and his K-9 partner performed a sniff of the vehicle's exterior, positively alerting to the presence of illegal drugs. We had the man and woman exit the vehicle, leaving the infant inside for safety reasons.

The woman protested saying that it was not possible to have drugs inside her car. The male suspect remained silent. She caught onto his silence and began to yell at him saying that there had better not be any drugs inside of her car.

Unfortunately for her, we found a fairly large quantity of crack cocaine in a plastic bag stuck down between the seats. When we showed it to her, she went ballistic, screaming at the male suspect who had still not said a word.

We separated the two of them so we could interview them separately. I truly believed she was unaware that the male suspect, the father of her child had hidden the crack cocaine in her car when we conducted the traffic stop. Yet, I am not so naieve as to believe that she didn't know he was a drug dealer, but women are pretty particular about having that sort of thing around their children.

Interviewing the male suspect off to the side, I explained that he and I both knew where the crack cocaine came from. His response, "I don't know anything about no crack cocaine."

I explained to him that he was going to be charged regardless, but unless he owned up to it, the mother of his child was going to be charged along with him. He still held to his story of not knowing anything about the drugs. I pushed harder explaining that if both he and the child's mother were arrested, the child would be taken by the department of social services. He still refused to own up to the crack cocaine we both knew he hid in the car.

My hands were tied. I had no choice but to arrest the child's mother and the suspect. You might ask, if I knew the crack cocaine belonged to the suspect and not the woman, why not let her go?

Well, as harsh as it may sound, what I know and what I can prove are usually two different things. If I were to let the mother go free, then the suspect would have a viable argument in court that the crack cocaine belonged to the mother and we had let her go. I didn't have any solid proof that the crack cocaine was the male suspect's. I didn't have a choice. Both were arrested and charged with a felony.

We had a marked unit transport the male suspect first and separate for a couple of reasons. First, I truly think that if they were in the back of the same patrol car, she would have tried to kill him. Second and maybe more importantly, I wanted to speak with her away from him.

As a consolation to her, I had her give me the number of a family member who could pick up her 6 month old son. I let her wait until they had arrived and allowed her to say goodbye to her son before she was taken to jail. It was the best I could offer her under the circumstances.

Clear as mud? It's not that hard if you think about it. Do you see how this all works? The bottom line: Be careful who you let into your vehicle and be careful whose vehicle you get into. That was shameful what that man put his child and the child's mother through all to protect himself, but it happens more than you know.

Recording Devices

This is really a no brainer. Always assume that when you are dealing with the police that everything you say or do is being recorded. The truth is that it is being recorded.

Today, the police have mobile cameras on the dashboards of their police cars. Some are equipped with reverse cameras as well. Officers wear digital transmitters that record the audio of any conversation they have with the public, some of which are fairly obvious and others not so much. Police cars are usually equipped with microphones in the back seat area to record your conversation once you have been arrested or detained.

All of this is completely legal. Obviously, you do not have an expectation of privacy while seated in the back of a patrol car. As far as the face to face recording, as long as one party knows it is happening, it is legal. The officer is that one person. A lot of departments require their officers to announce to you that you are being recorded. However, this announcement is usually done very fast and slipped into other parts of the conversation such as the introduction that most people don't even hear it. In addition, it is usually only an internal policy rather than a legal requirement. So, whether they announce to you the fact that they are recording your encounter or not will probably not matter in the resolution of your case.

The point is to be careful. Anything that is gleamed from these recordings is admissible in court. This is not just for proof of criminal activity, but it can also be admitted to the court to show your demeanor and attitude toward the officer at the time of the encounter. Nothing is more embarrassing than to have you appear on a video showing your butt and acting all out of control, especially when you are trying to appear professional in court.

On the flip side of this, if you believe there is evidence that may support your case recorded by the officer, you are well within your rights to request that evidence be admitted to court.

Just keep in mind, that once the genie is out of the bottle, he can't be put back in. Be aware of what you say and utilize your right to remain silent whenever possible. Remember, the only people truly on your side in a criminal matter are you and your lawyer.

Arguing Your Case in the Field

Do yourself a favor and do not argue your case with the police while you are still in the field. In most situations, the police officer has already made up his mind on what he is going to do. Second, the side of the road is not the place to hold court.

Save all of your arguments for the time when you are in front of a judge or a jury. Throwing yourself on the mercy of the officer can still be done in court. Save your dignity and wait for the appropriate time to mount your defense. On the street is not the time, nor the place.

Rather than trying your case in the field, you should do the same thing that the police are doing, trying to obtain as much information about your case as possible. Know the time of the day, note everything the officer says and does, note if there are any witnesses to the incident, and take mental notes of everything that you can.

As soon as you get a chance, write everything down on paper while your memory is still fresh. That is exactly what the police do. They write a report detailing everything that happened up to and including your arrest. They know that by the time your case reaches trial they are probably not going to remember all of the little details that can make or break a case. The difference is that they are writing from their perspective.

You need to follow their lead and do the same thing, but from your perspective. All of this information is invaluable when it comes time to defend you in court. Make good use of your energy and start preparing your case from the moment your encounter the police. Don't waste your time making arguments that are not going to get you anywhere and cause you to miss important details that could help you later.

To make your plea of innocence while sitting in the back of a patrol car in handcuffs is pointless. You also need to consider that if you start making your arguments before you are even arrested, you may be giving the police that last little bit they need to make their case.

We have court rooms, judges, and juries for a reason. Save your arguments for court.

3

Courtroom Procedure

As long as you haven't lived in a cave somewhere, you have undoubtedly seen your share of police and courtroom dramas on television or in the movies. Most everyone has a pretty good idea of what happens in a courtroom setting. The difference is that most of the examples you see on television or in the movies are more glamorous than real life. They are often cases involving life or death or some great conspiracy. Otherwise, we probably wouldn't watch, right?

Nonetheless, the same procedures and rights apply to every case in the criminal justice system, whether you are on trial for murder or speeding. Obviously with a case involving life and death, I would strongly suggest you have a lawyer and I think most everyone would agree with that statement. However, in cases of smaller magnitude, you do not always require a lawyer to represent you, even though you are entitled to one if you choose.

Of course, I cannot and will not tell you which way to go with that. It is completely your decision depending on the magnitude of your case and your comfort level in mounting a legal self-defense. In either event, this next section describes the general environment in all criminal court proceedings, what you can expect, and how to work within the system.

Pre-Trial Negotiation

Just like in the movies and on television, virtually every trial is preceded by some level of pre-trial negotiation. Depending on the size of the jurisdiction, the police officer himself may be acting as the prosecutor. In other jurisdictions, the city or county may have prosecutors that are handling the case. Yet, even if a prosecutor is handling your case, they are probably handling everyone who has court that day. Unless you are charged with a felony, this is usually the situation with traffic court or local court proceedings.

Yet, no matter how significant or insignificant your case is, the prosecution is almost always available in some way to negotiate your charge before it goes before a judge or a jury. Think about it, the prosecutor is facing a ton of cases. If they can negotiate some sort of plea with you that makes you both happy, then they save time and a lot of work.

I would argue that more than 95% of cases are resolved in pre-trial negotiations and a relatively small number actually go to trial. Just consider what would happen to our already overburdened court system that is backlogged with cases waiting to go to trial if things were reversed and every case went to the judge or a jury. The system would grind to a screeching halt. A purest would argue that every case should be tried regardless of the consequences or backlog that would be created, but that is just not a practical solution. So, pre-trial negotiations will continue to play a huge role in our criminal justice system and you need to take advantage of that.

Now, when you enter into a pre-trial negotiation, it might be something as simple as standing in the corner of the courtroom or off to the side talking to the officer about your case. Or, it may be a more formal process where you are called forward to speak with the officer and/or the prosecutor. Whichever way it goes, you must understand that this is a negotiation and in any negotiation compromise is usually the key to success, meaning that both sides need to come away with something.

For example, in a speeding case, maybe you don't want the points on your license but are willing to pay a higher fine or visa-versa. The officer or the prosecutor might be willing to accept that kind of plea agreement in that they get to close the case with a guilty plea and you get to have no points or no fine. Everyone wins and justice rules the day.

Maybe, you are in a situation where you have multiple traffic tickets such as speeding, no driver's license, and no proof of insurance. During the pre-trial negotiation, you may come to an agreement where you plead guilty to one of the charges outright and the others are dismissed.

Of course, I cannot promise that this is what will happen or your chances of success in a pre-trial negotiation. However, what I can promise is that it will not hurt you to go to court and try. Things never get worse than what they are. If you were charged with driving 20mph over the speed limit, it doesn't get worse by your going or not going to court. You have nothing to lose and everything to gain.

Quite frankly, it is foolish not go to court. As we have said before, the police and prosecutors are human. Like you and everyone else, they don't want to be tied up in court for hours dealing with minor infractions of the law either. They are almost always willing to work some sort of compromise in order to avoid going to trial and taking up more of their time for minor violations. Go to court and see what happens. If you can't come to an agreement with the officer and/or prosecutor, you can still go to trial.

Your Right to a Trial

I hate to keep using the television and Hollywood references to our criminal justice system, but it is arguably, the most written about and dramatized aspect of life in our country. Think of the number of television shows and theatrical movies about the police, our court system, and crime in our country. So, I continue to reference this as a foundation of your knowledge in what we are about to discuss and then build from there.

Under the 6th Amendment, you are guaranteed the right to a trial by a jury of your peers. This is usually the type of case that you see depicted on television or in the movies. Yet, just because it is a guaranteed right, it does not mean that you have to exercise it. For example, most small court criminal justice cases are resolved at what is called a Bench Trial. This is where you and the prosecution present your arguments and evidence directly to a judge. Then, he decides your guilt or innocence and what your punishment shall be. Again, this is done for the sake of timeliness in a court system already backed up with huge case loads. It takes a lot of time to poll a jury, seat them, and then prosecute a case. In addition, they generally do not use the same jury for multiple cases.

So, for example, in court today, there are ten speeding cases to be tried. If each of them were to go to a jury trial, then each would be entitled to poll their own jury, seat them, and then present their case. The jury selection process alone would most likely kill the day and all ten speeding cases would never get heard.

No matter what the charge or what the normal court procedure is in your jurisdiction, you are always guaranteed the right to a trial by a jury. It is your choice to make. No one can take that away from you.

Consider this, as we have spoken already about the time involved in prosecuting a case, regardless of its magnitude, the time that is required to poll and seat a jury, and the fact that the prosecution doesn't usually want to be there anymore than you do, pre-trial negotiations are a really big deal.

With all of that being said thus far, I also want you to consider this: Your guaranteed right to a trial by jury is another tool that you can use in your defense and negotiation.

For example, you have been charged with speeding and you go to court to resolve your case. You meet the prosecution in a pre-trial negotiation, but fail to come to an agreement, causing your case to go to trial. You can then elect to have your case tried by a jury. This does a couple of things.

First, it allowed you the chance to mediate your case with the prosecution in a pre-trial negotiation. Second, when the negotiation failed, your election of a trial by a jury buys you time to regroup and plan the next steps in your defense. It is highly unlikely that your jury trial is going to happen that very day. Your case will be rescheduled to a later date, almost always a month or longer out into the future. During that time, the officer's memory fades, the trial roster gets more and more backed up, and the prosecution is less thrilled about having to spend a day in court to win your speeding case.

Now, this is not necessarily a tactic that will earn you a dismissal of your charges, though that does happen. Instead, you are trying to force the prosecution back to the negotiation table to work out your case rather than go to trial. It's just a strategy.

Now, I am not saying to employ this strategy in every case. It all depends. You may want to go ahead and proceed with a Bench Trial. The reason I used speeding as the example before is that while arguments can surely be made, is it a much more difficult and technical case to argue. You stand a better chance of winning that type of case in front of a jury rather than a judge. Most of the members of a jury have driven in excess of the speed limit at some time or another, whether they were caught or not. They are likely to be more sympathetic to your case than a judge will be.

However, if you have a strong case and an argument to be made, sometimes it is better to just go before the judge in a Bench Trial. You only have to convince one person of your innocence as opposed to an entire jury. Then, your case is over and you can move on with your life. Either way, it is your decision to make and it can be a very valuable strategic tool if employed correctly.

The main thing that I want you to get out of this discussion is that you always have the right to a trial by jury, regardless of the type of case against you and regardless of the forum court is held in. It is your right, guaranteed by the 6th Amendment of the constitution. The choice is always yours.

Before we move on though, I must throw in one caveat to this. Once you decide which way you want to go with your case, you are locked in. You cannot select to have your case prosecuted as a Bench Trial, realize that maybe things are not going the way you want and then decide to have a Jury Trial instead. In addition, you certainly cannot wait to see the result of one form of trial, bench or jury, and then demand to be tried differently because you don't like the result. Once you choose one type of trial over the other, you are locked into it.

The Process

Again as most of you are probably already semi qualified as television lawyers and familiar with the courtroom scene, juries, witnesses, and the last moment heated confession from the stand, I am going to first move into the process of a Bench Trial, something seldom show on television or in the movies. While it follows the same general format, it is a much simpler process and from there we will build into the more complex Jury Trial.

The Bench Trial

As we have already outlined, a Bench Trial is between you and the prosecution in front of a judge. It is about as straight forward a process as it can get, but there are rules that you need to know and things that can help you to be successful. Let's go through a trial one step at a time.

First, the clerk of court calls your case. You and the prosecution approach the bench and move into your respective areas from which you will make your arguments. Any witnesses that either side have usually come forward and sit with the side for which they are going to testify. Now, every court room is different and some are more formal than others. Regardless, both sides have their respective areas from which they will proceed to make their arguments.

Next, the clerk of court or the judge himself will read the charges against you and ask if you understand them. After you acknowledge your understanding of the charges, you will be asked to enter a plea, guilty or not guilty.

Assuming you have come this far, this is where you would say "Not Guilty. However, I have seen some defendants get to this point and plead guilty to the charges, throwing their self onto the mercy of the court. I am not totally sure why they do this. I can only think that they were not happy with the result from their pre-trial negotiation and are hoping the judge will offer a better deal...? To me, if you have gotten to the point of standing before the judge or jury, it's time to make your arguments.

After you have entered your plea of not guilty, the judge will have anyone who is going to testify in the case, raise their right hand and swear or affirm that any testimony that is to be given is "the whole truth and nothing but the truth", after which the judge will initiate the case by turning it over to the prosecution to begin testimony.

Again, as we talked about earlier, the prosecutor may be a lawyer or it may be the police officer himself. In any event, with the judge having turned it over to the prosecution to begin the trial, they will make the first move. It only makes sense that they go first because they are the reason you are there. You didn't arrest yourself and just decide to spend your free time in court. It is the prosecution's responsibility to outline their case against you.

So, the police officer, acting as the prosecution or just the main witness in the case, outlines the state's case against you. It is and should be very specific. The date and time of the alleged incident, the specific facts of the case, the crime for which you were arrested and charged, the elements of that specific crime, and the probable cause the officer had for making the arrest should all be presented in great detail. The elements of the crime are extremely important and I will give you an example in just a little bit to illustrate why.

This next part is extremely important, and most people miss it when they are trying to defend themselves in court. After the police officer has finished testifying to the facts of the case, the judge will look to you and ask if you would like to question the witness. Let me say that again, the judge will look to you and ask if you would like to question the witness. Do I need to say it a third time?

This is not where you tell your story or your version of events or testify. You have the right under the 6th Amendment to confront your accusers. This means that you have the right to question anyone who gives testimony against you in your case. Use this right to your advantage. Ask the officer or any other witness for that matter questions about their testimony, their experience, or anything else that might be relevant to winning your case. You never know what you might learn or what errors you may discover that can mean the difference between a guilty and a not guilty verdict.

Too often, I have watched defendants in court, chomping at the bit to tell their side of the story, fail to ask any questions. Be patient. You will have that opportunity. But, use the rights you have been granted under the constitution. Do not squander them.

From a strategic point of view, you should already have questions prepared that you want to ask and a strategy in mind to win your case. Even if you don't have a strategy or pre-planned questions, take notes on what the police officer or other witnesses have testified to and ask questions. Let me say it again, ask questions.

You may find inconsistencies in what they have said or inconsistencies with the facts of your case, all of which can help to create a reasonable doubt as to your guilt. That is all you need to win, reasonable doubt, just a reasonable chance that you are innocent. They, on the other hand, have to prove your guilt beyond any reasonable doubt, or about 100 percent. You can learn a lot by asking questions. It is your right to do so and it may help you win your case. So, take advantage of it.

After you have finished asking the prosecution witness questions, also called cross examining the witness, the judge will ask the prosecution to present their next witness. Then, the process repeats itself.

Again, when given the chance to question the witness, take it. Once the prosecution has presented all of its witnesses and you have had the opportunity to question them, the case moves onto your argument.

This is the time where you have the opportunity to call upon your own witnesses and to testify to your side of events. Keep in mind, you hope to have made a strong enough case and possibly undermined the prosecution's case enough to avoid having to testify yourself.

Remember, just like you had the opportunity to question the prosecution's witnesses, they also have to right to question yours including any testimony you give. The process works both ways, anything that you testify to can be questioned and undermined by the prosecution. So try to make your case before it is your turn to present witnesses or give testimony.

Sometimes it is necessary to give testimony and call your own witnesses. Thus, the process is the same as it was for the prosecution. You may call upon any witnesses to testify on your behalf and you may testify yourself. After each has given their testimony, the judge will look to the prosecution and ask if they have any questions for the witness. It is the same process we just did when the prosecution presented their case and their witnesses. So, make sure to keep this in mind. Once someone gives testimony, they are fair game to be questioned by the other side.

After all the witnesses have been presented and all testimony has been given, you will have the chance to make a closing argument, basically giving the reasons that the prosecution has failed to make their case against you and the reasons for which you should be found not guilty. Usually, the prosecution goes first in this regard, giving all the reasons why you should be found guilty and then you get the last word to make your final statement.

After this the judge looks at all the facts that have been presented and the arguments that have been made by both sides, and renders a decision.

Once the judge makes his decision, and if you are found guilty, he will then pronounce the sentence. All of this sounds pretty dramatic, but in reality it is just the punishment for the crime you have been already been charged with and the punishment is usually already predetermined in the form of a fine.

In most of these Bench Trial level cases, the fine is pre-determined and is written on your citation. However, the judge has the power to set aside the fine, reduce the fine, break it into payments, etc. However, they generally do not have the power to increase the fine from its preset amount.

Usually, when an officer writes a citation and arrests a person, the fines charged for a crime are already preset by the court or the state at their maximum level. So, I am not trying to take away from a judge's power. As we have already said that they are the gods of their universe, but the fines are already set to the maximum. This is why I said that things can't get worse by going to court and pleading your case. You have nothing to lose and everything to gain.

Earlier in our discussion of Bench Trials, I said that I was going to give an example of a case where the defendant understood court room procedure, asked his questions, and made his arguments. Let me tell you that story here and it should really help to illustrate the entire process we have just discussed.

The case was called forward for a Bench Trial. The judge read off the charge of "Drinking (alcoholic beverage) in Public" and asked the defendant if he understood the charge. The defendant stated that he did. The judge asked him whether he was pleading guilty or not guilty. The defendant entered a plea of not guilty. The police officer, assisted by a city prosecutor and the defendant were sworn in. The judge then directed his attention to the prosecution, telling them to go forward with the facts of the case.

The police officer stated that on a given night and at a given time he responded to a call of a several disorderly individuals who were refusing to leave a bar. Upon his arrival, the bar manager indicated that the four individuals had left the establishment just seconds before and were last seen walking down the sidewalk.

Leaving the bar, the officer observed the four individuals walking down the sidewalk and away from the establishment. The officer approached the individuals to find out what had happened and investigate the incident further.

Upon stopping the four individuals, the officer observed that one of the four individuals had an open full bottle of beer in his hand. The officer placed this individual under arrest for "Drinking in Public". As no other charges could be made on the remaining three individuals, they were released without further action or incident.

The individual with the open full bottle of beer was charged with "Drinking in Public", was transported to the city jail and was processed. This individual is the defendant appearing in court today.

Sound pretty straight forward? A cut and dry case, or is it?

The judge then directed his attention to the defendant and asked if he had any questions for the police officer. The defendant said that he did and the judge directed the defendant to proceed with his questions.

The defendant turned to the officer and began asking him questions. He started by rehashing the basic details of the call itself, the time of day, how many people the officer observed at the bar, and how many people the officer had observed on the sidewalk as he approached the four alleged disorderly individuals.

Then, he asked the officer at what point had he observed the defendant with an open bottle of beer in his hand. The police officer said he could see that the defendant had what appeared to be an open bottle of beer in his hand from the moment he left the bar and begun walking toward the defendant and the other three individuals.

Then, the defendant asked at what point was the officer able to confirm his suspicions that the item in the defendant's hand was truly an open bottle of beer. The officer replied that it became clear that the item was an open bottle of beer when he stopped the defendant and the other three individuals. The defendant asked the officer if any of the other three individuals were in possession of any open bottles of beer. The police officer said that they were not.

Next, the defendant asked the officer if, during the entire time he had watched the defendant up until the time he was placed under arrest, had he observed the defendant drink from the open bottle of beer. The police officer stated that he had not. The defendant concluded his questioning of the police officer.

How do things look now? How would you find in this case?

At this point the judge asked the defendant if he had any witnesses that he would like to present or if he would like to give testimony to the incident. The defendant answered negative to both questions.

Then, the judge asked the prosecution if they had any closing remarks that they would like to make. They said, no. Then, the judge asked the defendant if he had any closing statements he would like to make. The defendant said, yes.

In his closing statement, the defendant said that while he did in fact leave the bar with an open full bottle of beer in his possession, and walk down the public sidewalk with that beer, at no time did he ever consume any of the beer from the bottle. The defendant went on to state, even based on the officer's testimony itself, he was never observed drinking the beer in a public place.

He stated that he had just purchased the beer from the bar, when he and his three friends were asked to leave. He admittedly took the just purchased beer with him, intending to drink it when he returned to his hotel room rather than poor it out or leave it behind in the bar.

He finished his closing statement by reciting the elements of the "Drinking in Public" violation which specifically included the "consumption of alcoholic beverage in a public place". As he had not drank from the beer bottle nor was he observed by anyone consuming alcoholic beverage in a public place, he argued that he could not be found guilty of the charge of Drinking in Public.

The judge scratched his head and looked at the police officer, asking if he had any rebuttal argument. The police officer did not. Without further testimony or argument to be presented, the judge stated that if the defendant had been charged with "Open Container of an Alcoholic

Beverage" it might be a different story. Yet, as charged, the prosecution failed to prove the defendant had violated the law in question. Therefore, based on the facts of the case, the judge found the defendant not guilty.

Surprise you? Maybe or maybe not. Do you see how the process works?

The point is that the defendant in this case did a little bit of homework, prepared a strategy, and made an argument. While this is not a high crime by any stretch of the imagination, the criminal justice system works along the same principles at every level.

From the peanut gallery observing this case while I waited for one of my own to be called, I almost wanted to cheer for the defendant. I guess I am a different type of police officer. I like the debate and the argument. When my cases can hold up under scrutiny and I win guilty verdicts, it shows me that I am doing a good job. When I lose, as was the officer's situation here, I learn from my mistakes and it helps me to be a better police officer in future cases. Not all the police feel or think the way I do. The officer in this case was quite unhappy with the verdict, but if he had made the correct charge to begin with he might have won. Hopefully he learned from his mistake and will be better for it.

Something else I want you to take notice of in this example, the defendant never gave direct testimony. He didn't have too. That was also very smart on his part. Though the prosecution was given the opportunity to rebut the arguments made in the defendant's closing statement, they were not allowed to question him directly because he had not given any testimony.

Remember, whenever you talk, you open yourself up to questions and scrutiny that can help the prosecution's case against you. Try to avoid that whenever you can. This defendant did an outstanding job in his case, but he is the exception.

Most people in his shoes would have gone to court and pled guilty, throwing themselves on the mercy of the court for their punishment. Or, they would have testified to all of the things the officer had already said without giving any new information or creating any doubt in the case, a waste of time.

Don't be that person. This entire book has been dedicated to giving you the basic tools to help you defend yourself in court. Be the defendant in this example and not the one throwing himself on the mercy of the court or rambling on in meaningless speech that only ends up supporting the prosecution's case. I am trying to get you to **think** before you act or speak. Do that alone, and your chances of success go up exponentially.

The Jury Trial

While a jury trial follows the same basic procedural rules as a bench trial, it can become significantly more complicated. Therefore, I would strongly recommend hiring a lawyer if you elect to take your case in this direction.

Even though everything from the Bench Trial holds true for a Jury Trial, the same cannot be said in reverse. The fact that a "jury" is involved is enough to make the process much more complex. A jury must be polled and seated. This means that from a pool of potential jurors, twelve must be selected to hear your case.

You and the prosecution have the right to question each potential juror. In addition, you and the prosecution have a limited number of no questions asked excusals. This means that you or the prosecution can excuse a potential juror from hearing your case for any reason.

Some of the most famous litigators in our country would say that cases are won and lost, not during the trial, but at jury selection. The process alone is pretty complex, but so are the strategies. Hire a lawyer.

With that said, I want to discuss the use of jury trials as a strategy for just a moment. We have already said that the 6th Amendment guarantees you the right to a trial by jury and it is your option to exercise that right or opt instead for a Bench Trial. In making this decision, you need to think about a few things.

As you will need to hire an attorney, is a Jury Trial worth the cost versus the charge and potential punishment you will face if found guilty? Maybe or maybe not.

I recommend a Jury Trial for speeding cases when you cannot reach an agreement during pre-trial negotiation. As we have already said, it is a tool to force the prosecution back to the negotiation table and leverage a better deal. Jury Trials cost the government money. If they are looking to fine you $200 for speeding, the cost of a jury trial including man-hours, preparatory filings, etc far exceed that amount. They would really rather not go that route.

You also need to consider your costs as well. If your maximum potential fine is $200, most lawyers charge well in excess of that per hour. Now, you can weigh that against the cost of your increased insurance rates as a result of a guilty verdict, but it will probably still not balance out.

So, while in some cases a Jury Trial is absolutely necessary, in others I would tend to think of it more as a tool and decide later if it is worth pursuing. You can always settle or plea your case up to the point of a verdict being handed down. If the government seems insistent on going all the way to trial, essentially calling your bluff, you have to decide how far you are willing to go and the cost effectiveness of the whole thing.

In trying to decide whether you should take your case to a Jury Trial, you should think about your audience. If your case involves something where you think you can get a jury to empathize with you, relate to your situation, then maybe it is the way to go.

Remember, a jury is made up of people just like you. Also consider that in a Bench Trial you only have to convince a judge. In a Jury Trial, you have twelve people to deal with. You only need one on your side to win your case, but peer pressure can be a big factor with jurors.

Despite the potential issues with a jury, there are a lot of advantages as well. For example, for the prosecution to obtain a guilty verdict from a jury, all twelve of the jury members must vote guilty. In order for you to win a not guilty verdict, you only need one jury member to vote not guilty. So, as far as the odds go, you only need to create a reasonable doubt in one of twelve jurors whereas the prosecution must create a certainty of guilt in all twelve.

The odds are greatly in your favor, but again a lot depends on the crime and the public's general feeling toward people committing the same violation as you.

While in a Jury Trial, the jurors have the responsibility of determining your guilt or innocence, the judge is only there to oversee the process and make sure that both the prosecution and the defense follow the rules. Pretty much everything else remains the same.

That's it in a nut shell. If you really intend on going forward into a Jury Trial, while you are not required to have a lawyer, I strongly urge that you do. Enough said. Let's move on.

General Strategies

When your case goes to court and you have unsuccessfully moved past the pre-trial negotiations, you must start to examine and prepare a strategy for your defense. There are several different ways that you can approach this and we will briefly discuss each of them.

Argue the Facts

This is probably the most difficult strategy to employ in your defense. Unless you have solid evidence that you can submit to the court to show that the evidence provided by the prosecution is wrong, it is an extreme uphill battle.

Unfortunately, a large number of defense lawyers follow this strategy. They receive the prosecution's case against you and all of their evidence. Then, they attempt to make arguments for each piece of the evidence in order to show that the prosecution's facts are wrong.

This is like playing catch up in a game where you are already in the hole. It's not that it cannot be done. But, I would suggest being a little more proactive in your defense. You can argue the facts of your case, but couple it with other strategies to increase your chance for success.

You need to make the strongest case you can, and not just try to show where the prosecution is wrong. You need to give the judge or the jury a reason to find you not guilty. It doesn't have to be a big reason, just a reason. That is why they say you must be convicted or found guilty within a shadow of a doubt.

You must create that shadow in the judge or the jury's mind and that cannot be done by arguing the prosecution's facts alone.

Discredit the Witness

While you may think that this is dirty pool so to speak, it is a very good strategy to employ. Depending on what you are charged with, the prosecution will endeavor to show you as the biggest offender out there and as someone who doesn't deserve the consideration of a not guilty verdict. So, it is what it is, a part of the game.

In a speeding case, your chance of winning based on proving a malfunction in the radar is futile at best. Your chance lies in showing that the radar operator was not qualified to run it or made mistakes in its operation.

For example, did the officer's department or state require him to be certified in the use and operation of the radar unit? Can he prove his current certification? Was the officer required to calibrate the radar unit and did he perform this action? Can he prove that he did so? On a side note, police officers do not calibrate their radar units. That is a highly technical process conducted by factory representatives at given intervals throughout the year. A police officer only checks the unit's calibration. If a police officer states that he calibrated his radar unit and did so regularly, he just demonstrated his lack of proficiency with the piece of equipment in its use and operation. You just undermined the witness.

But, I would not pounce on that just yet. Rather, keep building your case against the prosecution and pounce during your closing arguments. Anyway, you get the gist of what I am trying to say.

Let's quickly look at another example. In the "Drinking in Public" case, the defendant did not necessarily undermine the witness. Instead, he used the police officer's own words against him. Lawyers do that all the time.

All you need to do is create a level of doubt in the prosecution's case. Did the witness actually see what happened? Were they in a position to see or were they behind something or too far away to have actually witnessed the incident?

You don't have to be harsh or cruel, just ask the questions. Maybe, you can plant doubt in the witness' mind. Could it have been a bottle of soda rather than a beer? Could it have been a white car instead of a gray one? Is it possible from that distance and in that low light you might have seen something else?

If you can get the prosecution's witness to doubt themselves, you have just crossed a huge hurdle toward winning your case.

Blame Someone Else

Another great way to win a case is to give the jury someone else to blame. Now, this doesn't work in all cases. Obviously, if you are stopped and arrested for DUI, speeding, or other offenses like that, it is going to be pretty difficult to blame someone else when you were the one driving.

However, in another case where the prosecution is alleging that you committed shoplifting because you were captured on a grainy video committing the act, you were detained a while later away from the incident scene, but you were not in possession of the stolen items, the prosecution is going to rely on the video tape evidence and witness statements.

Did you know that among all of the different forms of evidence that can be used against you, witness statements are the most unreliable? This is a well proven and well documented fact.

In this situation, you could attempt to put forth a defense based on the idea that the police arrested the wrong guy. This doesn't mean you just stand there and say "It wasn't me."

You need to show how someone else could have reasonably been the one recorded in the video committing the crime and observed by witnesses. The fact that you were wearing the same color hooded sweatshirt and that you match the same general description of the suspect are certainly going to be presented by the prosecution as irrefutable evidence. Yet, is this really conclusive? Maybe, it's coincidental at best.

If you don't argue that point, then the jury will take what the prosecution gives them as being the gospel on the matter.

You need to argue the fact that the sweatshirt you were wearing is quite common. You can argue the number of people who live in the area and shop at the victim's store who similarly match your description. In essence, you are trying to undermine the prosecution's case by showing that the crime could have reasonably been committed by someone other than you.

That is all you need, create doubt in the jury's mind. If they have doubt, they cannot convict.

Innocence, To Prove or Not to Prove

It would certainly be nice to go into court and prove your innocence beyond a reasonable doubt. However, this is no small task to accomplish. Think about it. The prosecution has to convince the jury of your guilt beyond a reasonable doubt. They have the burden of proving your guilt to a certainty. All you have to do is create a doubt of your guilt. Why climb Mount Everest if you don't have to? That is the prosecution's problem.

Do not place the same heavy burden on yourself that the prosecution carries. Like I said before, it would be great to be able to go into court and throw it in everyone's face when you prove your innocence beyond a shadow of a doubt. However, at the end of the day, the goal is to be found not guilty. It doesn't matter by what margin, any not guilty verdict will do.

If you get too wrapped up in trying to prove your innocence, you may miss the boat and fail to even create reasonable doubt. Then, you lose. At the end of the day, you know whether you are innocent or guilty. Beyond that, it doesn't matter what anyone else thinks, only whether you are convicted of the crime. That is the end game here, a not guilty verdict.

Don't lose sight of your goal in all of this. Don't let your pride lead you into a guilty verdict. Not that your innocence doesn't matter, but in court it almost doesn't. Everything becomes a function of what can be proven. The prosecution is going to try and prove you are guilty of the crime. Your job is only to create doubt in that guilt, a reason for the judge or jury to dismiss the case. Do not overcomplicate things. Keep it simple.

Be the Prosecution

Thinking like the prosecution is obviously a fairly straight forward concept. There is nothing hidden here and no secret strategy. Simply, put yourself in the prosecutor's shoes. What would you do to win a guilty conviction if you were prosecuting your case?

When you start to think like your adversary, you will gain insight into what they may do and the strategies that they will use to win. Whenever I have ever dealt with a problem or an issue, I always try to look at it in a full 360 degrees. This means that I attempt to look at a problem from every possible angle. I don't like surprises.

The more ways I can look at a problem, the less likely I am to be surprised by something. Trust me, the last place and the most awkward time is when you are caught off guard in a courtroom. Someone says something completely unexpected, or you ask a question and are completely caught off guard by the answer you get. You don't want this to happen.

I heard a lawyer once say that you never ask a question for which you don't already know the answer. When you are planning your case and your defense, think about the questions you would ask if you were the prosecutor. Think about the different answers that might be given and how those answers can affect your overall case.

You also need to think about the questions you will ask and the possible answers you will receive. Don't assume that witnesses will always be honest in court. Similarly, don't assume that a witness is going to lie. Be prepared as best you can for any situation.

Ask yourself, how would I make the case against me? It will reveal holes and weaknesses in your defense. It can also give you hints to the strategies the prosecution may use against you and the potential holes in their case.

As a police officer, I have used this technique in interviews and in courtroom testimony. I am always prepared. Be prepared and your chances of winning increase exponentially. Playing things fast and loose or making up your strategy as you go is a recipe for disaster. The prosecution seldom makes this error, but defendants do, which leads to more guilty than not guilty verdicts.

The criminal justice system, particularly in the courtroom, is very similar to a game of chess. Every move has meaning and every question has a reason. Try to think and be at least a step ahead of the prosecution. In the end, it could mean the difference between your success and your failure.

Rules of Evidence

A Brady Motion

Technically, the prosecution is required by law to submit to you any and all evidence pertaining to your case, especially if the prosecution intends to use it in court. This can include the official police report, witness lists, video or audio recordings, witness statements, photographs, documentation and test results for any evidence gathered, documentation for the chain of custody of evidence, etc.

The list of items that the prosecution is required to provide to you is virtually endless. They are required by law to provide this information to you so that you may adequately prepare your defense. You are entitled to this information in any case you are involved in, from the most minor to the most serious of offenses.

As this information is upon what the prosecution is building their case, it is in your interest to see what they have. So, get the information.

If you have to file a formal request, there are any number of websites that can walk you through it using templates etc. to make the process easier. But, do get the information. It is a preview of what the prosecution intends to use against you.

Though the prosecution is required by law to provide this information to you, it doesn't hurt to file what is commonly known in legal circles as a Brady Motion. You may obtain assistance of a lawyer to file this motion with the prosecution, but you just as easily look it up on the internet to find a guide or utility to walk you through the process.

The legal system is very formal and runs on paper and protocol. While you are lawfully entitled to the information from your case, I would still suggest you file the motion anyway. It covers you in the event the prosecution tries to say that they never received a request.

Do everything by the book and keep copies of every correspondence you have with the prosecution. It may prove to be a great help should problems or questions arise during the court room proceedings.

The Submission of Evidence

You are not as stringently bound to tell the prosecution how you plan to defend yourself in court as they are in having to tell you what they plan to do. An exception to this may lie in their right to know who you may call as a witness only in that the prosecution is afforded the opportunity to present a rebuttal witness to counter any you put forth.

When it comes time for trial, the prosecution is not allowed to enter anything into evidence that you had not received prior notice of. This prevents them from holding back and dropping a bomb on you in the middle of court.

Now, prosecutors have been known to try that kind of strategy, but it is up to you to raise an objection to this kind of tactic. The judge will then make the decision to allow the evidence into the trial, exclude the evidence, or allow you the time to consider the evidence and reconvene court on another day.

Do not be afraid to object to any tactic that you feel is out of line. Give your reasons for your objection and let the judge make his decision. Sometimes your objection will stand and other times your objection may not be successful. Either way, you should never hesitate to raise an objection to something that you feel is out of line or improper.

Judges and lawyers both are very used to having objections raised. You are not going to hurt their feelings or make them mad. Besides, it is your butt on the line. So, who cares if they don't like your objecting to something they do.

If you have evidence that you want to submit to the court for consideration, advise the court of this fact at the time you plan to submit the evidence. The judge will acknowledge you and wait for any objection from the prosecution.

Do not just approach the judge and submit evidence. The last thing you want to do is make the judge angry with you. Remember, in a court of law, the judge is the god of the universe. You do not want to feel their wrath. Besides not being good for your case, it can prove to be a very uncomfortable experience as you are locked up for contempt of court.

Make sure that if you are submitting evidence to the court for consideration, you have enough copies when possible to present one to the judge, one to the prosecution, and one to show the jury or a witness. This works great for paper evidence that can be photocopied, but it is not always possible for other forms of evidence.

Do the best you can to be considerate and professional. While this may not go directly to your case, your conduct in court can have significant indirect consequences on your success or failure.

Be Professional

You don't have to be a lawyer to be professional in court. You may be just an average person with an average education. Yet, professionalism is reflected in how you dress, how you speak, and the level of resect you show for witnesses, the prosecution, and the judge. You don't have to like any of them, but you had better show common courtesy and respect.

Dress formally. Do not show up to court in a pair of shorts and a tank top shirt. Believe me, I have seen it. Address the police officer as "officer" or by their rank. Address the witnesses as "mam" or "sir". Address the prosecutor as "the prosecution", "the state or city", or as "counselor". Address the judge as "your honor".

Being respectful costs you nothing, but it can go a long way toward creating an atmosphere where the judge or the jury want to find on your behalf. Again, we have already talked about this, but in court it's not always about your actual guilt or innocence. In reality, it's a lot of little things that come together to make or break your case. The idea is to deal with the things in your power to control and argue those that you cannot.

Don't let something as simple as the way you dressed or the way you spoke to members of the court be the underlying reason you are found guilty. Even if you lose your case, a judge or a jury is often more inclined to be lenient on a defendant who was professional, respectful, and showed courtesy.

Do not lose your cool. You have to be virtually emotion free. If things are going your way and you are winning, hold it in. There will be plenty of time to celebrate later. If you are losing, hold it in. Showing a negative reaction will embolden the prosecution to move in for the kill because they know they hit a nerve. If not, they will at the very least go out of their way to exploit that nerve and try to make you lose your focus. Stay on target.

Always remember what the goal is, a not guilty verdict. None of this is hardly ever personal. It's all part of the game. Remember that.

4

Conclusion

Throughout this entire book, I have sought to provide you with a basic understanding of your rights, the processes of the criminal justice system, and court room procedures. Obviously, these are all very wide ranging topics to which entire books have been dedicated. It was never my intent to make anyone an expert. Rather, this book is intended to serve as a foundation on which you can build your knowledge and better prepare yourself for participation within the system.

With the information contained here, you should be much better equipped to handle an encounter with the police and to better defend yourself in court. You would never think of playing any sort of game without knowing the rules. How could you possibly win...?

This book has given you an overview of the rules for the game we call the criminal justice system. It is impossible to write an example for every possible situation. The examples given are intended to make you think and see how everything comes together in a real world setting. Thinking is the key to your success. You must know the rules and make a plan in order to be successful.

Always remember, knowledge is power. Never stop learning. The more you know, the better prepared you will be. Learning never stops. Research some of the issues we have discussed in this book and you will find even more in depth descriptions and examples of how these things all come together. Use your common sense and think about how you would prosecute your case if the roles were reversed. This alone may be the biggest key to your defense. It allows you to see things from the other side and better prepare your defense against it.

The easiest way to combat the criminal justice system is to stay out of trouble. Then, you will never have to use any of the tools we have discussed here. However, should you find yourself in a bad position, knowing your rights and the rules governing the criminal justice system will help you to successfully defend yourself.

I want to wish the best of luck in whatever situation you may find yourself. Though you are capable and legally entitled the right to defend yourself in court, if you ever have a doubt consult with an attorney. At the very least, you will be an educated client and better able to ensure success in your case.

Other Books in the Series

The Rules of the Game:
Strategies for Legal Defense in DUI Cases

ISBN-13: 978-1478313564
ISBN-10: 1478313560

The Rules of the Game:
Speeding and other Criminal Defenses

www.ingramcontent.com/pod-product-compliance
Lightning Source LLC
Chambersburg PA
CBHW030939180526
45163CB00002B/624